TERENCE RATTIGAN

Born in 1911, a scholar at Harrow and at Trinity College, Oxford, Terence Rattigan had his first long-running hit in the West End at the age of twenty-five: *French Without Tears* (1936). His next play, *After the Dance* (1939), opened to euphoric reviews yet closed under the gathering clouds of war, but with *Flare Path* (1942) Rattigan embarked on an almost unbroken series of successes, with most plays running in the West End for at least a year and several making the transition to Broadway: *While the Sun Shines* (1943), *Love in Idleness* (1944), *The Winslow Boy* (1946), *The Browning Version* (performed in double-bill with *Harlequinade*, 1948), *Who is Sylvia?* (1950), *The Deep Blue Sea* (1952), *The Sleeping Prince* (1953) and *Separate Tables* (1954). From the mid-fifties, with the advent of the 'Angry Young Men', he enjoyed less success on stage, though *Ross* (1960) and *In Praise of Love* (1973) were well received. As well as seeing many of his plays turned into successful films, Rattigan wrote a number of original plays for television from the fifties onwards. He was knighted in 1971 and died in 1977.

**Other titles by the same author
published by Nick Hern Books**

After the Dance

The Browning Version and *Harlequinade*

Cause Célèbre

The Deep Blue Sea

First Episode

Flare Path

In Praise of Love

Love in Idleness / Less Than Kind

Rattigan's Nijinsky
(adapted from Rattigan's screenplay by Nicholas Wright)

Separate Tables

Who is Sylvia? and *Duologue*

The Winslow Boy

Terence Rattigan

FRENCH WITHOUT TEARS

Introduced by
Dan Rebellato

NICK HERN BOOKS
London

www.nickhernbooks.co.uk

A Nick Hern Book

This edition of *French Without Tears* first published in Great Britain in 1995 by Nick Hern Books, The Glasshouse, 49a Goldhawk Road, London W12 8QP by arrangement with Methuen. *French Without Tears* was included in Volume One of *The Collected Plays of Terence Rattigan* published in 1953 by Hamish Hamilton

Printed in this edition in 2015, in association with the Orange Tree Theatre, London

Typeset by Country Setting, Kingsdown, Kent CT14 8ES
Printed in the UK by Mimeo Ltd, Huntingdon, Cambridgeshire PE29 6XX

A CIP catalogue record for this book is available from the British Library

ISBN 978 1 84842 524 8

Terence Rattigan (1911–1977)

Terence Rattigan stood on the steps of the Royal Court Theatre, on 8 May 1956, after the opening night of John Osborne's *Look Back in Anger*. Asked by a reporter what he thought of the play, he replied, with an uncharacteristic lack of discretion, that it should have been retitled 'Look how unlike Terence Rattigan I'm being.' [1] And he was right. The great shifts in British theatre, marked by Osborne's famous première, ushered in kinds of playwriting which were specifically unlike Rattigan's work. The pre-eminence of playwriting as a formal craft, the subtle tracing of the emotional lives of the middle classes – those techniques which Rattigan so perfected – fell dramatically out of favour, creating a veil of prejudice through which his work even now struggles to be seen.

Terence Mervyn Rattigan was born on 10 June 1911, a wet Saturday a few days before George V's coronation. His father, Frank, was in the diplomatic corps and Terry's parents were often posted abroad, leaving him to be raised by his paternal grandmother. Frank Rattigan was a geographically and emotionally distant man, who pursued a string of little-disguised affairs throughout his marriage. Rattigan would later draw on these memories when he created Mark St Neots, the bourgeois Casanova of *Who is Sylvia?* Rattigan was much closer to his mother, Vera Rattigan, and they remained close friends until her death in 1971.

Rattigan's parents were not great theatregoers, but Frank Rattigan's brother had married a Gaiety Girl, causing a minor family uproar, and an apocryphal story suggests that the 'indulgent aunt' reported as taking the young Rattigan to the theatre may have been this scandalous relation.[2] And when, in the summer of 1922, his family went to stay in the country cottage of the drama critic Hubert Griffiths, Rattigan avidly worked through his extensive library of playscripts. Terry went to Harrow in 1925, and there maintained both his somewhat illicit theatregoing habit and his insatiable reading, reputedly devouring every play in the school library. Apart from contemporary authors like Galsworthy, Shaw and Barrie, he also read the plays of Chekhov, a writer whose crucial influence he often acknowledged.[3]

His early attempts at writing, while giving little sign of his later sophistication, do indicate his ability to absorb and reproduce his own theatrical experiences. There was a ten-minute melodrama about the Borgias entitled *The Parchment*, on the cover of which the author recommends with admirable conviction that a suitable cast for this work might comprise 'Godfrey Tearle, Gladys Cooper, Marie Tempest, Matheson Lang, Isobel Elsom, Henry Ainley . . . [and] Noël Coward'.[4] At Harrow, when one of his teachers demanded a French playlet for a composition exercise, Rattigan, undaunted by his linguistic shortcomings, produced a full-throated tragedy of deception, passion and revenge which included the immortal curtain line: 'COMTESSE. (*Souffrant terriblement.*) Non! non! non! Ah non! Mon Dieu, non!'[5] His teacher's now famous response was 'French execrable: theatre sense first class'.[6] A year later, aged fifteen, he wrote *The Pure in Heart,* a rather more substantial play showing a family being pulled apart by a son's crime and the father's desire to maintain his reputation. Rattigan's ambitions were plainly indicated on the title pages, each of which announced the author to be 'the famous playwrite and author T. M. Rattigan.'[7]

Frank Rattigan was less than keen on having a 'playwrite' for a son and was greatly relieved when in 1930, paving the way for a life as a diplomat, Rattigan gained a scholarship to read History at Trinity, Oxford. But Rattigan's interests were entirely elsewhere. A burgeoning political conscience that had led him to oppose the compulsory Officer Training Corps parades at Harrow saw him voice pacifist and socialist arguments at college, even supporting the controversial Oxford Union motion 'This House will in no circumstances fight for its King and Country' in February 1933. The rise of Hitler (which he briefly saw close at hand when he spent some weeks in the Black Forest in July 1933) and the outbreak of the Spanish Civil War saw his radical leanings deepen and intensify. Rattigan never lost his political compassion. After the war he drifted towards the Liberal Party, but he always insisted that he had never voted Conservative, despite the later conception of him as a Tory playwright of the establishment.[8]

Away from the troubled atmosphere of his family, Rattigan began to gain in confidence as the contours of his ambitions and his identity moved more sharply into focus. He soon took advantage of the university's theatrical facilities and traditions. He joined The Oxford Union Dramatic Society (OUDS), where contemporaries included Giles Playfair, George Devine, Peter Glenville, Angus Wilson and Frith Banbury. Each year, OUDS ran a one-act play competition and in Autumn 1931 Rattigan submitted one. Unusually, it seems that this was a highly experimental effort, somewhat like Konstantin's piece in *The Seagull.* George Devine, the OUDS president, apparently told the young author, 'Some of it is absolutely smashing, but it goes too far'.[9] Rattigan was instead to make his first mark as a somewhat scornful reviewer for the student newspaper, *Cherwell,* and as a performer in the Smokers (OUDS's private revue club), where he adopted the persona and dress of 'Lady Diana Coutigan', a drag performance which allowed him to discuss leading members of the Society with a barbed camp wit.[10]

That the name of his Smokers persona echoed the contemporary phrase, 'queer as a coot', indicates Rattigan's new-found confidence in his homosexuality. In February 1932, Rattigan played a tiny part in the OUDS production of *Romeo and Juliet*, which was directed by John Gielgud and starred Peggy Ashcroft and Edith Evans (women undergraduates were not admitted to OUDS, and professional actresses were often recruited). Rattigan's failure to deliver his one line correctly raised an increasingly embarrassing laugh every night (an episode which he re-uses to great effect in *Harlequinade*). However, out of this production came a friendship with Gielgud and his partner, John Perry. Through them, Rattigan was introduced to theatrical and homosexual circles, where his youthful 'school captain' looks were much admired.

A growing confidence in his sexuality and in his writing led to his first major play. In 1931, he shared rooms with a contemporary of his, Philip Heimann, who was having an affair with Irina Basilevich, a mature student. Rattigan's own feelings for Heimann completed an eternal triangle that formed the basis of the play he co-wrote with Heimann, *First Episode*. This play was accepted for production in Surrey's 'Q' theatre; it was respectfully received and subsequently transferred to the Comedy Theatre in London's West End, though carefully shorn of its homosexual subplot. Despite receiving only £50 from this production (and having put £200 into it), Rattigan immediately dropped out of college to become a full-time writer.

Frank Rattigan was displeased by this move, but made a deal with his son. He would give him an allowance of £200 a year for two years and let him live at home to write; if at the end of that period, he had had no discernible success, he would enter a more secure and respectable profession. With this looming deadline, Rattigan wrote quickly. *Black Forest*, an O'Neill-inspired play based on his experiences in Germany in 1933, is one of the three that have survived. Rather unwillingly, he collaborated with Hector Bolitho on an adaptation of the latter's novel, *Grey Farm*, which received a disastrous New York production in 1940. Another project was an adaptation of *A Tale of Two Cities*, written with Gielgud; this fell through at the last minute when Donald Albery, the play's potential producer, received a complaint from actor-manager John Martin-Harvey who was beginning a farewell tour of his own adaptation, *The Only Way*, which he had been performing for forty-five years. As minor compensation, Albery invited Rattigan to send him any other new scripts. Rattigan sent him a play provisionally titled *Gone Away*, based on his experiences in a French language Summer School in 1931. Albery took out a nine-month option on it, but no production appeared.

By mid-1936, Rattigan was despairing. His father had secured him a job with Warner Brothers as an in-house screenwriter, which was reasonably paid; but Rattigan wanted success in the theatre, and his desk-bound life at Teddington Studios seemed unlikely to advance this ambition. By chance, one of Albery's productions was unexpectedly losing money, and the wisest course of action seemed to be to pull the show and replace it with something cheap. Since *Gone Away* required a relatively small cast and only one set, Albery quickly arranged for a production. Harold French, the play's director, had only one qualm: the title. Rattigan suggested *French Without Tears*, which was immediately adopted.

After an appalling dress rehearsal, no one anticipated the rapturous response of the first-night audience, led by Cicely Courtneidge's infectious laugh. The following morning Kay Hammond, the show's female lead, discovered Rattigan surrounded by the next day's reviews. 'But I don't believe it', he said. 'Even *The Times* likes it.' [11]

French Without Tears played over 1000 performances in its three-year run and Rattigan was soon earning £100 a week. He moved out of his father's home, wriggled out of his Warner Brothers contract, and dedicated himself to spending the money as soon as it came in. Partly this was an attempt to defer the moment when he had to follow up this enormous success. In the event, both of his next plays were undermined by the outbreak of war.

After the Dance, an altogether more bleak indictment of the Bright Young Things' failure to engage with the iniquities and miseries of contemporary life, opened, in June 1939, to euphoric reviews; but only a month later the European crisis was darkening the national mood and audiences began to dwindle. The play was pulled in August after only sixty performances. *Follow My Leader* was a satirical farce closely based on the rise of Hitler, co-written with an Oxford contemporary, Tony Goldschmidt (writing as Anthony Maurice in case anyone thought he was German). It suffered an alternative fate. Banned from production in 1938, owing to the Foreign Office's belief that 'the production of this play at this time would not be in the best interests of the country', [12] it finally received its première in 1940, by which time Rattigan and Goldschmidt's mild satire failed to capture the real fears that the war was unleashing in the country.

Rattigan's insecurity about writing now deepened. An interest in Freud, dating back to his Harrow days, encouraged him to visit a psychiatrist that he had known while at Oxford, Dr Keith Newman. Newman exerted a svengali-like influence on Rattigan and persuaded the pacifist playwright to join the RAF as a means of curing his writer's block. Oddly, this unorthodox treatment seemed to have some effect; by 1941, Rattigan was writing again. On one dramatic sea crossing, an engine failed, and with everyone forced to jettison all excess baggage and possessions, Rattigan threw the hard covers and blank pages from the notebook containing his new play, stuffing the precious manuscript into his jacket.

Rattigan drew on his RAF experiences to write a new play, *Flare Path*. Bronson Albery and Bill Linnit who had both supported *French Without Tears* both turned the play down, believing that the last thing that the public wanted was a play about the war.[13] H. M. Tennent Ltd., led by the elegant Hugh 'Binkie' Beaumont, was the third management offered the script; and in 1942, *Flare Path* opened in London, eventually playing almost 700 performances. Meticulously interweaving the stories of three couples against the backdrop of wartime uncertainty, Rattigan found himself 'commended, if not exactly as a professional playwright, at least as a promising apprentice who had definitely begun to learn the rudiments of his job'.[14] Beaumont, already on the way to becoming the most powerful and successful West End producer of the era, was an influential ally for Rattigan. There is a curious side-story to this production; Dr Keith Newman decided to watch 250 performances of this play and write up the insights that his 'serial attendance' had afforded him. George Bernard Shaw remarked that such playgoing behaviour 'would have driven me mad; and I am not sure that [Newman] came out of it without a slight derangement'. Shaw's caution was wise.[15] In late 1945, Newman went insane and eventually died in a psychiatric hospital.

Meanwhile, Rattigan had achieved two more successes; the witty farce, *While the Sun Shines*, and the more serious, though politically clumsy, *Love in Idleness* (retitled *O Mistress Mine* in America). He had also co-written a number of successful films, including *The Day Will Dawn, Uncensored, The Way to the Stars* and an adaptation of *French Without Tears*. By the end of 1944, Rattigan had three plays running in the West End, a record only beaten by Somerset Maugham's four in 1908.

Love in Idleness was dedicated to Henry 'Chips' Channon, the Tory MP who had become Rattigan's lover. Channon's otherwise gossipy diaries record their meeting very discreetly: 'I dined with Juliet Duff in her little flat . . . also there, Sibyl Colefax and Master Terence Rattigan, and we sparkled over the Burgundy. I like Rattigan enormously, and feel a new friendship has begun. He has a flat in Albany'.[16] Tom Driberg's rather less discreet account fleshes out the story: Channon's 'seduction of the playwright was almost like the wooing of Danaë by Zeus – every day the playwright found, delivered to his door, a splendid present – a case of champagne, a huge pot of caviar, a Cartier cigarette-box in two kinds of gold . . . In the end, of course, he gave in, saying apologetically to his friends, 'How can one *not?*' '.[17] It was a very different set in which Rattigan now moved, one that was wealthy and conservative, the very people he had criticised in *After the*

Dance. Rattigan did not share the complacency of many of
his friends, and his next play revealed a deepening complexity and
ambition.

For a long time, Rattigan had nurtured a desire to become
respected as a serious writer; the commercial success of *French
Without Tears* had, however, sustained the public image of
Rattigan as a wealthy young light comedy writer-about-town. [18]
With *The Winslow Boy*, which premièred in 1946, Rattigan began
to turn this image around. In doing so he entered a new phase as a
playwright. As one contemporary critic observed, this play 'put
him at once into the class of the serious and distinguished
writer'.[19] The play, based on the Archer-Shee case in which a
family attempted to sue the Admiralty for a false accusation of
theft against their son, featured some of Rattigan's most elegantly
crafted and subtle characterization yet. The famous second curtain,
when the barrister Robert Morton subjects Ronnie Winslow to a
vicious interrogation before announcing that 'The boy is plainly
innocent. I accept the brief', brought a joyous standing ovation on
the first night. No less impressive is the subtle handling of the
concept of 'justice' and 'rights' through the play of ironies which
pits Morton's liberal complacency against Catherine Winslow's
feminist convictions.

Two years later, Rattigan's *Playbill*, comprising the one-act plays
The Browning Version and *Harlequinade*, showed an ever
deepening talent. The latter is a witty satire of the kind of touring
theatre encouraged by the new Committee for the Encouragement
of Music and Arts (CEMA, the immediate forerunner of the Arts
Council). But the former's depiction of a failed, repressed Classics
teacher evinced an ability to choreograph emotional subtleties on
stage that outstripped anything Rattigan had yet demonstrated.

Adventure Story, which in 1949 followed hard on the heels of
Playbill, was less successful. An attempt to dramatize the
emotional dilemmas of Alexander the Great, Rattigan seemed
unable to escape the vernacular of his own circle, and the epic
scheme of the play sat oddly with Alexander's more prosaic
concerns.

Rattigan's response to both the critical bludgeoning of this play
and the distinctly luke-warm reception of *Playbill* on Broadway
was to write a somewhat extravagant article for the *New
Statesman*. 'Concerning the Play of Ideas' was a desire to defend
the place of 'character' against those who would insist on the pre-
eminence in drama of ideas.[20] The essay is not clear and is couched
in such teasing terms that it is at first difficult to see why it should
have secured such a fervent response. James Bridie, Benn Levy,
Peter Ustinov, Sean O'Casey, Ted Willis, Christopher Fry and
finally George Bernard Shaw all weighed in to support or condemn
the article. Finally Rattigan replied in slightly more moderate

terms to these criticisms insisting (and the first essay reasonably supports this) that he was not calling for the end of ideas in the theatre, but rather for their inflection through character and situation.[21] However, the damage was done (as, two years later, with his 'Aunt Edna', it would again be done). Rattigan was increasingly being seen as the arch-proponent of commercial vacuity.[22]

The play Rattigan had running at the time added weight to his opponents' charge. Originally planned as a dark comedy, *Who is Sylvia?* became a rather more frivolous thing both in the writing and the playing. Rattled by the failure of *Adventure Story*, and superstitiously aware that the new play was opening at the Criterion, where fourteen years before *French Without Tears* had been so successful, Rattigan and everyone involved in the production had steered it towards light farce and obliterated the residual seriousness of the original conceit.

Rattigan had ended his affair with Henry Channon and taken up with Kenneth Morgan, a young actor who had appeared in *Follow My Leader* and the film of *French Without Tears*. However, the relationship had not lasted and Morgan had for a while been seeing someone else. Rattigan's distress was compounded one day in February 1949, when he received a message that Morgan had killed himself. Although horrified, Rattigan soon began to conceive an idea for a play. Initially it was to have concerned a homosexual relationship, but Beaumont, his producer, persuaded him to change the relationship to a heterosexual one.[23] At a time when the Lord Chamberlain refused to allow any plays to be staged that featured homosexuality, such a proposition would have been a commercial impossibility. The result is one of the finest examples of Rattigan's craft. The story of Hester Collyer, trapped in a relationship with a man incapable of returning her love, and her transition from attempted suicide to groping, uncertain self-determination is handled with extraordinary economy, precision and power. The depths of despair and desire that Rattigan plumbs have made *The Deep Blue Sea* one of his most popular and moving pieces.

1953 saw Rattigan's romantic comedy *The Sleeping Prince*, planned as a modest, if belated, contribution to the Coronation festivities. However, the project was hypertrophied by the insistent presence of Laurence Olivier and Vivien Leigh in the cast and the critics were disturbed to see such whimsy from the author of *The Deep Blue Sea*.

Two weeks after its opening, the first two volumes of Rattigan's *Collected Plays* were published. The preface to the second volume introduced one of Rattigan's best-known, and most notorious creations: Aunt Edna. 'Let us invent,' he writes, 'a character, a nice respectable, middle-class, middle-aged, maiden lady, with time on her hands and the money to help her pass it'.[24] Rattigan paints a picture of this eternal theatregoer, whose bewildered disdain for modernism ('Picasso—'those dreadful reds, my dear, and why three noses?'')[25] make up part of the particular challenge of dramatic writing. The intertwined commercial and cultural pressures that the audience brings with it exert considerable force on the playwright's work.

Rattigan's creation brought considerable scorn upon his head. But Rattigan is neither patronizing nor genuflecting towards Aunt Edna. The whole essay is aimed at demonstrating the crucial rôle of the audience in the theatrical experience. Rattigan's own sense of theatre was *learned* as a member of the audience, and he refuses to distance himself from this woman: 'despite my already self-acknowledged creative ambitions I did not in the least feel myself a being apart. If my neighbours gasped with fear for the heroine when she was confronted with a fate worse than death, I gasped with them'.[26] But equally, he sees his job as a writer to engage in a gentle tug-of-war with the audience's expectations: 'although Aunt Edna must never be made mock of, or bored, or befuddled, she must equally not be wooed, or pandered to or cosseted'.[27] The complicated relation between satisfying and surprising this figure may seem contradictory, but as Rattigan notes, 'Aunt Edna herself is indeed a highly contradictory character'.[28]

But Rattigan's argument, as in the 'Play of Ideas' debate before it, was taken to imply an insipid pandering to the unchallenging expectations of his audience. Aunt Edna dogged his career from that moment on and she became such a by-word for what theatre should *not* be that in 1960, the Questors Theatre, Ealing, could title a triple-bill of Absurdist plays, 'Not For Aunt Edna'.[29]

Rattigan's next play did help to restore his reputation as a serious dramatist. *Separate Tables* was another double-bill, set in a small Bournemouth hotel. The first play develops Rattigan's familiar themes of sexual longing and humiliation while the second pits a man found guilty of interfering with women in a local cinema against the self-appointed moral jurors in the hotel. The evening was highly acclaimed and the subsequent Broadway production a rare American success.

However, Rattigan's reign as the leading British playwright was about to be brought to an abrupt end. In a car from Stratford to London, early in 1956, Rattigan spent two and a half hours informing his Oxford contemporary George Devine why the new play he had discovered would not work in the theatre. When Devine persisted, Rattigan answered 'Then I know nothing about plays'. To which Devine replied, 'You know everything about plays, but you don't know a fucking thing about *Look Back in Anger*.' [30] Rattigan only barely attended the first night. He and Hugh Beaumont wanted to leave at the interval until the critic T. C. Worsley persuaded them to stay.[31]

The support for the English Stage Company's initiative was soon overwhelming. Osborne's play was acclaimed by the influential critics Kenneth Tynan and Harold Hobson, and the production was revived frequently at the Court, soon standing as the banner under which that disparate band of men (and women), the Angry Young Men, would assemble. Like many of his contemporaries, Rattigan decried the new movements, Beckett and Ionesco's turn from Naturalism, the wild invective of Osborne, the passionate socialism of Wesker, the increasing influence of Brecht. His opposition to them was perhaps intemperate, but he knew what was at stake: 'I may be prejudiced, but I'm pretty sure it won't survive,' he said in 1960, 'I'm prejudiced because if it *does* survive, I know I won't.' [32]

Such was the power and influence of the new movement that Rattigan almost immediately seemed old-fashioned. And from now on, his plays began to receive an almost automatic panning. His first play since *Separate Tables* (1954) was *Variation on a Theme* (1958). But between those dates the critical mood had changed. To make matters worse, there was the widely publicized story that nineteen year-old Shelagh Delaney had written the successful *A Taste of Honey* in two weeks after having seen *Variation on a Theme* and deciding that she could do better. A more sinister aspect of the response was the increasingly open accusation that Rattigan was dishonestly concealing a covert homosexual play within an apparently heterosexual one. The two champions of Osborne's play, Tynan and Hobson, were joined by Gerard Fay in the *Manchester Guardian* and Alan Brien in the *Spectator* to ask 'Are Things What They Seem?' [33]

When he is not being attacked for smuggling furtively homosexual themes into apparently straight plays, Rattigan is also criticized for lacking the courage to 'come clean' about his sexuality, both in his life and in his writing.[34] But neither of these criticisms really hit the mark. On the one hand, it is rather disingenuous to suggest that Rattigan should have 'come out'. The 1950s were a difficult time for homosexual men. The flight to the Soviet Union of Burgess and Maclean in 1951 sparked off a major witch-hunt against homosexuals, especially those in prominent positions. Cecil Beaton and Benjamin Britten were rumoured to be targets.[35] The police greatly stepped up the investigation and entrapment of homosexuals and prosecutions rose dramatically at the end of the forties, reaching a peak in 1953-54. One of their most infamous arrests for importuning, in October 1953, was that of John Gielgud.[36]

But neither is it quite correct to imply that somehow Rattigan's plays are *really* homosexual. This would be to misunderstand the way that homosexuality figured in the forties and early fifties. Wartime London saw a considerable expansion in the number of pubs and bars where homosexual men (and women) could meet. This network sustained a highly sophisticated system of gestural and dress codes, words and phrases that could be used to indicate one's sexual desires, many of them drawn from theatrical slang. But the illegality of any homosexual activity ensured that these codes could never become *too* explicit, *too* clear. Homosexuality, then, was explored and experienced through a series of semi-hidden, semi-open codes of behaviour; the image of the iceberg, with the greater part of its bulk submerged beneath the surface, was frequently employed.[37] And this image is, of course, one of the metaphors often used to describe Rattigan's own playwriting.

Reaction came in the form of a widespread paranoia about the apparent increase in homosexuality. The fifties saw a major drive to seek out, understand, and often 'cure' homosexuality. The impetus of these investigations was to bring the unspeakable and underground activities of, famously, 'Evil Men' into the open, to make it fully visible. The Wolfenden Report of 1957 was, without doubt, a certain kind of liberalizing document in its recommendation that consensual sex between adult men in private be legalized. However the other side of its effect is to reinstate the integrity of those boundaries – private/public, hidden/exposed, homosexual/heterosexual – which homosexuality was broaching. The criticisms of Rattigan are precisely part of this same desire to divide, clarify and expose.

Many of Rattigan's plays were originally written with explicit homosexual characters (*French Without Tears*, *The Deep Blue Sea* and *Separate Tables*, for example), which he then changed.[38] But many more of them hint at homosexual experiences and activities: the relationship between Tony and David in *First Episode*, the Major in *Follow my Leader* who is blackmailed over an incident in Baghdad ('After all,' he explains, 'a chap's only human, and it was a deuced hot night –'),[39] the suspiciously polymorphous servicemen of *While the Sun Shines*, Alexander the Great and T. E. Lawrence from *Adventure Story* and *Ross*, Mr Miller in *The Deep Blue Sea* and several others. Furthermore, rumours of Rattigan's own bachelor life circulated fairly widely. As indicated above, Rattigan always placed great trust in the audiences of his plays, and it was the audience which had to decode and reinterpret these plays. His plays cannot be judged by the criterion of 'honesty' and 'explicitness' that obsessed a generation after Osborne. They are plays which negotiate sexual desire through structures of hint, implications and metaphor. As David Rudkin has suggested, 'the craftsmanship of which we hear so much loose talk seems to me to arise from deep psychological necessity, a drive to organize the energy that arises out of his own pain. Not to batten it down but to invest it with some expressive clarity that speaks immediately to people, yet keeps itself hidden'.[40]

The shifts in the dominant view of both homosexuality and
the theatre that took place in the fifties account for the brutal
decline of Rattigan's career. He continued writing, and while
Ross (1960) was reasonably well received, his ill-judged musical
adaptation of *French Without Tears*, *Joie de Vivre* (1960), was
a complete disaster, not assisted by a liberal bout of laryngitis
among the cast, and the unexpected insanity of the pianist.[41] It
ran for four performances.

During the sixties, Rattigan was himself dogged with ill-health:
pneumonia and hepatitis were followed by leukaemia. When his
death conspicuously failed to transpire, this last diagnosis was
admitted to be incorrect. Despite this, he continued to write,
producing the successful television play *Heart to Heart* in 1962,
and the stage play *Man and Boy* the following year, which
received the same sniping that greeted *Variation on a Theme*. In
1964, he wrote *Nelson – a Portrait in Miniature* for Associated
Television, as part of a short season of his plays.

It was at this point that Rattigan decided to leave Britain and live
abroad. Partly this decision was taken for reasons of health; but
partly Rattigan just seemed no longer to be welcome. Ironically, it
was the same charge being levelled at Rattigan that he had faced
in the thirties, when the newspapers thundered against the those
who had supported the Oxford Union's pacifist motion as 'woolly-
minded Communists, practical jokers and sexual indeterminates'.[42]
As he confessed in an interview late in his life, 'Overnight almost,
we were told we were old-fashioned and effete and corrupt and
finished, and . . . I somehow accepted Tynan's verdict and went
off to Hollywood to write film scripts'.[43] In 1967 he moved to
Bermuda as a tax exile. A stage adaptation of his Nelson play, as
Bequest to the Nation, had a luke-warm reception.

Rattigan had a bad sixties, but his seventies seemed to indicate a
turnaround in his fortunes and reputation. At the end of 1970, a
successful production of *The Winslow Boy* was the first of ten
years of acclaimed revivals. In 1972, Hampstead Theatre revived
While the Sun Shines and a year later the Young Vic was praised
for its *French Without Tears*. In 1976 and 1977 *The Browning
Version* was revived at the King's Head and *Separate Tables* at
the Apollo. Rattigan briefly returned to Britain in 1971, pulled
partly by his renewed fortune and partly by the fact that he was
given a knighthood in the New Year's honours list. Another
double bill followed in 1973: *In Praise of Love* comprised the
weak *Before Dawn* and the moving tale of emotional concealment
and creativity, *After Lydia*. Critical reception was more respectful
than usual, although the throwaway farce of the first play
detracted from the quality of the second.

Cause Célèbre, commissioned by BBC Radio and others,
concerned the Rattenbury case, in which Alma Rattenbury's aged

husband was beaten to death by her eighteen-year-old lover. Shortly after its radio première, Rattigan was diagnosed with bone cancer. Rattigan's response, having been through the false leukaemia scare in the early sixties, was to greet the news with unruffled elegance, welcoming the opportunity to 'work harder and indulge myself more'.[44] The hard work included a play about the Asquith family and a stage adaptation of *Cause Célèbre*, but, as production difficulties began to arise over the latter, the Asquith play slipped out of Rattigan's grasp. Although very ill, he returned to Britain, and on 4 July 1977, he was taken by limousine from his hospital bed to Her Majesty's Theatre, where he watched his last ever première. A fortnight later he had a car drive him around the West End where two of his plays were then running before boarding the plane for the last time. On 30 November 1977, in Bermuda, he died.

As Michael Billington's perceptive obituary noted, 'his whole work is a sustained assault on English middle class values: fear of emotional commitment, terror in the face of passion, apprehension about sex'.[45] In death, Rattigan began once again to be seen as someone critically opposed to the values with which he had so long been associated, a writer dramatizing dark moments of bleak compassion and aching desire.

Notes

1. Quoted in Rattigan's *Daily Telegraph* obituary (1 December 1977).

2. Michael Darlow and Gillian Hodson. *Terence Rattigan: The Man and His Work*. London and New York: Quartet Books, 1979, p. 26.

3. See, for example, Sheridan Morley. 'Terence Rattigan at 65.' *The Times*. (9 May 1977).

4. Terence Rattigan. Preface. *The Collected Plays of Terence Rattigan: Volume Two*. London: Hamish Hamilton, 1953, p. xv.

5. *Ibid.,* p. viii.

6. *Ibid.,* p. vii.

7. *Ibid.*, p. vii.

8. cf. Sheridan Morley, *op. cit.*

9. Humphrey Carpenter. *OUDS: A Centenary History of the Oxford University Dramatic Society*. With a Prologue by Robert Robinson. Oxford: Oxford University Press, 1985, p. 123.

10. Rattigan may well have reprised this later in life. John Osborne, in his autobiography, recalls a friend showing him a picture of Rattigan performing in an RAF drag show: 'He showed me a photograph of himself with Rattigan, dressed in a *tutu*, carrying a wand, accompanied by a line of aircraftsmen, during which Terry had sung his own show-stopper, 'I'm just about the oldest fairy in the business. I'm quite the oldest fairy that you've ever seen".' John Osborne. *A Better Class of Person: An Autobiography, Volume I 1929-1956*. London: Faber and Faber, 1981, p. 223.

11. Darlow and Hodson *op. cit.*, p. 83.

12. Norman Gwatkin. Letter to Gilbert Miller, 28 July 1938. in: *Follow My Leader*. Lord Chamberlain's Correspondence: LR 1938. [British Library].

13. Richard Huggett. *Binkie Beaumont: Eminence Grise of the West Theatre 1933-1973*. London: Hodder & Stoughton, 1989, p. 308.

14. Terence Rattigan. Preface. *The Collected Plays of Terence Rattigan: Volume One*. London: Hamish Hamilton, 1953, p. xiv.

15. George Bernard Shaw, in: Keith Newman. *Two Hundred and Fifty Times I Saw a Play: or, Authors, Actors and Audiences*. With the facsimile of a comment by Bernard Shaw. Oxford: Pelagos Press, 1944, p. 2.

16. Henry Channon. *Chips: The Diaries of Sir Henry Channon*. Edited by Robert Rhodes James. Harmondsworth: Penguin, 1974, p. 480. Entry for 29 September 1944.

17. Tom Driberg. *Ruling Passions*. London: Jonathan Cape, 1977, p. 186.

18. See, for example, Norman Hart. 'Introducing Terence Rattigan,' *Theatre World*. xxxi, 171. (April 1939). p. 180 or Ruth Jordan. 'Another Adventure Story,' *Woman's Journal*. (August 1949), pp. 31-32.

19. Audrey Williamson. *Theatre of Two Decades*. New York and London: Macmillan, 1951, p. 100.

20. Terence Rattigan. 'Concerning the Play of Ideas,' *New Statesman and Nation*. (4 March 1950), pp. 241-242.

21. Terence Rattigan. 'The Play of Ideas,' *New Statesman and Nation*. (13 May 1950), pp. 545-546. See also Susan Rusinko, 'Rattigan versus Shaw: The 'Drama of Ideas' Debate'. in: *Shaw: The Annual of Bernard Shaw Studies: Volume Two*. Edited by Stanley Weintraub. University Park, Penn: Pennsylvania State University Press, 1982. pp. 171-78.

22. John Elsom writes that Rattigan's plays 'represented establishment writing'. *Post-War British Drama*. Revised Edition. London: Routledge, 1979, p. 33.

23. B. A. Young. *The Rattigan Version: Sir Terence Rattigan and the Theatre of Character*. Hamish Hamilton: London, 1986, pp. 102-103; and Darlow and Hodson, *op. cit.*, p. 196, 204n.

24. Terence Rattigan. *Coll. Plays: Vol. Two. op. cit.*, pp. xi-xii.

25. *Ibid.*, p. xii.

26. *Ibid.*, p. xiv.

27. *Ibid.*, p. xvi.

28. *Ibid.*, p. xviii.

29. Opened on 17 September 1960. cf. *Plays and Players*. vii, 11 (November 1960).

30. Quoted in Irving Wardle. *The Theatres of George Devine*. London: Jonathan Cape, 1978, p. 180.

31. John Osborne. *Almost a Gentleman: An Autobiography, Volume II 1955-1966*. London: Faber and Faber, 1991, p. 20.

32. Robert Muller. 'Soul-Searching with Terence Rattigan.' *Daily Mail*. (30 April 1960).

33. The headline of Hobson's review in the *Sunday Times*, 11 May 1958.

34. See, for example, Nicholas de Jongh. *Not in Front of the Audience: Homosexuality on Stage*. London: Routledge, 1992, pp. 55-58.

35. Kathleen Tynan. *The Life of Kenneth Tynan*. Corrected Edition. London: Methuen, 1988, p. 118.

36. Cf. Jeffrey Weeks. *Coming Out: Homosexual Politics in Britain from the Nineteenth Century to the Present*. Revised and Updated Edition. London and New York: Quartet, 1990, p. 58; Peter Wildeblood. *Against the Law*. London: Weidenfeld and Nicolson, 1955, p. 46. The story of Gielgud's arrest may be found in Huggett, *op. cit.*, pp. 429-431. It was Gielgud's arrest which apparently inspired Rattigan to write the second part of *Separate Tables*, although again, thanks this time to the Lord Chamberlain, Rattigan had to change the Major's offence to a heterosexual one. See Darlow and Hodson, *op. cit.*, p. 228.

37. See, for example, Rodney Garland's novel about homosexual life in London, *The Heart in Exile*. London: W. H. Allen, 1953, p. 104.

38. See note 36; and also 'Rattigan Talks to John Simon,' *Theatre Arts*. 46 (April 1962), p. 24.

39. Terence Rattigan and Anthony Maurice. *Follow my Leader*. Typescript. Lord Chamberlain Play Collection: 1940/2. Box 2506. [British Library].

40. Quoted in Darlow and Hodson, *op. cit.,* p. 15.

41. B. A. Young, *op. cit.,* p. 162.

42. Quoted in Darlow and Hodson, *op. cit.,* p. 56.

43. Quoted in Sheridan Morley, *op. cit.*

44. Darlow and Hodson, *op. cit.,* p. 308.

45. *Guardian*. (2 December 1977).

French Without Tears

In 1934, Terence Rattigan was convinced that he was a playwright. Two years later, he was wondering if anything he wrote would ever be performed again.

The modest success of his first play, *First Episode*, had encouraged him to pursue an entirely immodest lifestyle. Despite investing £200 in the transfer and having received only £100 in return, it seemed clear to him that he was now a successful West End playwright. He gave this news to his father, dropped out from Oxford, and moved to London. Most of March and April 1934 were spent partying and dining out, relying on friends and betting on horses to finance his new lifestyle. His father urged him to move back home, and when *First Episode* closed late in April Rattigan soberly complied. A deal was struck whereby Rattigan would be given an allowance for two years, after which, if no signs of a playwriting career had manifested themselves, he would follow his father into the Diplomatic Service.

Rattigan wrote play after play at his desk upstairs at Stanhope Gardens. One piece was called *Black Forest*, described by its author as 'a turgid drama about tangled emotions'. Drawing on a trip to Germany in the summer of 1933, the play concerns a schoolteacher and his family on holiday in the Black Forest, whose members become entangled with an expelled ex-pupil of the father's school and the boy's German lover. Even given Rattigan's characteristic harsh judgement of his own work, the play's rejection by every management that read it is not entirely surprising.

Of five other plays written during this period only three have survived: an adaptation of *A Tale of Two Cities*, written with John Gielgud, another of Hector Bolitho's novel, *Grey Farm*, which Rattigan's equal measures of disdain both for the book and its author made rather onerous. The third surviving play was initially titled, *Joie de Vivre*, then *French Chalk* and thirdly, *Gone Away*.

In summer 1931, Frank Rattigan, at that point still envisaging a diplomatic career for his son, had sent Terry to a crammer in Wimereux, near Boulogne, to get his French up to an acceptable standard. The school was run by M. Martin, a formidable character, whose disdain for Rattigan's remarkable linguistic inadequacies was continually broadcast, usually at the communal house meals where only French could be spoken. 'Ah, Mon Dieu!'

he would daily cry, 'Entendez, Messieurs, cette nouvelle abomination de Monsieur Rottingham!' Years later, Rattigan recalled, 'It was an all-male environment and all we did was gossip away to each other in English. I learned no French whatever'.[1] *Gone Away* was a farce, based on his experience of this crammer. On holiday in Exmouth with his parents, Rattigan wrote the play in four weeks, writing it straight out in a school exercise-book and then typing it with two fingers: 'There was no time to make any corrections. The play went out just as I'd written it'.[2] However, this play, too, remained adamantly unperformed. Nine producers in all turned the script down.

When a production of *A Tale of Two Cities* fell through in the late summer of 1935 (see p. vii), the West End producer, Bronson Albery, consoled the young writer by offering to read any other scripts he had. Rattigan hesitated on which piece to offer until his mother took charge: 'Better let him read a good farce than a bad drama!'[3] Rattigan sent off *Gone Away* and, to his surprise, Albery took out a nine-month option on the script. Rattigan's initial delight gave way to dismay as it became clear that Albery did not see the project as a priority and by the summer of 1936, the option had lapsed with no sign of a production.

Rattigan's period of grace with his father had also elapsed, but Frank Rattigan gave his son one more chance and secured a screenwriting job for him at Teddington Studios, working for Warner Brothers. Under the system then operating, Warner Brothers would hire writers on lengthy, renewable contracts, during the period of which they could be hired out at inflated rates to other studios, Warner Brothers pocketing the difference.[4] The work was mechanical, the scripts formulaic, but Rattigan was in no position to refuse. Although he was now earning regular money, he found the work frustrating. The first script he completed was torn up in front of his eyes by the studio head, Irving Asher, who called in another scriptwriter and said, 'I want you to take this young man Terence Rattigan away, and show him how to write scripts *properly*'.[5]

However, the period with Warner Brothers was not entirely without value. The discipline of the studio's approach to writing gave Rattigan an opportunity to develop further his sense of dramatic structure. And one of Rattigan's co-workers at Teddington, the novelist, Anthony Powell, recalls: 'Over a period of about three weeks Terry Rattigan and I were immured together with the purpose of producing a story between us. This brief collaboration added no classic to movie history, indeed professionally speaking, was totally barren, but we laughed a lot over preposterous subjects discussed as possibilities'.[6] Working alongside other aspiring writers, and with the security of a regular wage, Rattigan's later successes with scripts like *The Way to the Stars, Brighton Rock,*

The Yellow Rolls Royce and *Goodbye Mr Chips* can be traced back to the intensive training he received at Teddington.

At one point, Rattigan even offered world rights for *Gone Away* to Warner Brothers for £200. Fortunately for him they refused, because at the Criterion Theatre, Albery's new project, *The Lady of La Paz*, was faltering. It would be two months before a new major production would be ready, so he cast around for a cheap, stop-gap to fill the theatre. Gielgud reminded him of *Gone Away*, which with its single set and small, young cast fitted Albery's requirements, and Rattigan was informed that his play would at last open at the Criterion in November, though after a mere two weeks of rehearsal and no out-of-town try-out.

The director, Harold French, had just completed a film contract when he ran into the actress, Kay Hammond, at the Café de Paris. She informed him that he was about the receive a script from Albery: "He's sending it to your club. I'm going to be in it and it's very funny." The way she accented 'very' defied me to think otherwise,' he recalls.[7] Happily, French concurred with Hammond's verdict, also admiring a quality of tenderness that complemented the play's farcical energy.

When he met Albery the next morning, French discovered that Kay Hammond, Jessica Tandy, Percy Walsh and Robert Flemyng had already been cast. He was also told to go and see a young actor called Rex Harrison in *Heroes Don't Care* (a farce set on a polar expedition) at St. Martin's Theatre, to consider him for the part of Alan. He and Hammond went to see the production and were both won over by the lightness and elegance of his performance. Rattigan's agent, A. D. Peters, who put up some of the money for the production, recommended for the part of Kenneth the then unknown Trevor Howard, who had understudied at Stratford during the previous season. The part of Rogers, the Naval Commander, was more difficult to fill, and eventually French took a risk with Roland Culver, a film actor he had worked with before, but who, with his 'bald head and oddly gesticulating hands', was mainly known for playing villains.[8]

Like Hammond, Culver was delighted by the play when he read it, but Harrison was more circumspect. He knew that his stock was rising and was uncertain that this 'nice cheerful little play' would showcase him adequately.[9] Nonetheless he eventually agreed. The top salary was £25 per week, and Harrison asked for £30. He did not get it, but since he was under contract to Alexander Korda, who would therefore be taking a percentage of his salary, he was given a small percentage of the box office, as was Jessica Tandy, the only *bona fide* star in the whole production.

Rattigan played very little part in the casting, as was usual then; indeed, he played a minor role in the entire rehearsal process.

French recalls how at the first read-through,

> I noticed a character sitting in the far corner of the room, well
> outside the semi-circle. Sometimes he chuckled, and once or
> twice seemed to be making a note. I imagined he must be an
> assistant stage manager making a list of 'props' that he would
> have to find. At the end of the second act, coffee was served. It
> was then that I asked Kay if she knew who the odd man out
> was. Her eyes opened even wider than usual!
>
> 'Oh darling, hasn't anybody introduced you? That's the
> author.' She took me by the hand and performed a belated
> introduction. I found myself talking to a tall, slim youngster to
> whom no one had thought it necessary to offer a cup of coffee.
> He seemed quite overwhelmed when I managed to produce a
> cup and thrust it into his hand.

The read-through itself was unremarkable; Culver and Hammond
read rather badly, and the play's wit made only momentary
appearances. Afterwards, French took Rattigan to the Green
Room, a theatrical club in central London. Rattigan spent the
evening, gazing star-struck at the actors and directors milling past
him, 'as though,' said French, 'he believed dreams could come
true'.[10] French made a number of suggestions concerning the play,
which Rattigan happily accepted; as he admitted later, he was 'so
enslaved by my director's charm that he could have asked me to
change Rex Harrison's part into a Rumanian Prince disguised as a
Nubian belly dancer and I would have cordially agreed'.[11] The
only remaining problem was the title, which French did not like;
Rattigan promised to think about it and after French had got
home, at 1.30 in the morning, he received an apologetic phone call
from Rattigan bashfully offering a new title: *French Without
Tears*. French immediately agreed.

The title was not the only change made in the play during the
rehearsal process. The famous joke in the opening moments of the
play ('*elle a des idées au-dessus de sa gare*') was added by
Rattigan during rehearsals. More substantially, the actor who had
originally been cast as Brian, Alec Archdale, was not working out,
and he was replaced by Guy Middleton. Substituting an actor
some way into rehearsals is difficult enough, but this was
complicated by the fact that Guy Middleton was at the time
having an affair with Rex Harrison's wife, Collette. In the event,
Harrison had had a series of extra-marital affairs himself, and his
marriage was pretty much over. Worried about 'the figure he
would cut in court as a cuckold', Harrison remained cool but
cordial with Middleton throughout rehearsals.[12]

The last major change was one which prefigured similar changes Rattigan would also make in *The Deep Blue Sea* and *Separate Tables*. At the end of the play, the temptress, Diana, eagerly awaits the arrival of Lord Heybrook, hoping to make him her next catch:

> *The* OTHERS *crowd round window.* KIT *goes to door at back.*
>
> KIT. (*Calling*) Diana! Lord Heybrook!
>
> JACQUELINE. (*Leaning over* ALAN's *shoulder*.) What does he look like, Alan?
>
> ALAN. I can't see. Your father's in the way.
>
> *The* CROWD *round the window disperses as a taxi-man comes in, carrying two suitcases.* MAINGOT *follows.*
>
> MAINGOT. (*To taximan*). Apportez-les en haut. Tenez. Je vous montrerai sa chambre. (*Calling*) Par ici, Milord.
>
> LORD HEYBROOK *comes in. He is a pale, slender man, with golden hair. He has a Borzoi on a lead.*
>
> MAINGOT. D'abord je vous montrerai votre chambre. Les presentations après.
>
> *He opens door at back.* LORD HEYBROOK *goes towards it. Before he reaches it,* DIANA *comes in in a bathing dress and wrap. She flashes him a brilliant smile, but he appears not to notice her.*
>
> LORD HEYBROOK. (*To the Borzoi, sibilantly*) Come along, Alcibiades. Follow your master.
>
> *He goes out.* MAINGOT *and the taximan follow.* JACQUELINE *collapses with laughter on* KIT's *chest. The* OTHERS *begin to laugh also.*[13]

This ending caused problems at the dress rehearsal, when the Borzoi dog grew fonder of a table leg than the Lord Chamberlain would have allowed. More substantially, Rattigan had begun to feel that this use of an easy stereotype to get a laugh left an 'unpleasant taste', would kill the lines immediately after it, and was 'out of character with the rest of the play'.[14] In its place, Rattigan had realised that since titles could be inherited at any age, Lord Heybrook could easily be revealed as a young boy. But as this conversation was taking place after the first dress rehearsal, it was now very late to make such a substantial change (to say nothing of the fact that George Astley, the actor hired to play Lord Heybrook, had dyed his hair specially for the part). Albery was sure to refuse.

And indeed he was not pleased. But cheered that one child actor was considerably cheaper than an adult actor and a hired Borzoi

dog, he assented. A few further changes were required before the
second dress rehearsal – Rex Harrison's costume was comically
small, the cast carried out their moves as if startled by the
furniture, and Roland Culver's wig appeared not of this world –
but everything was otherwise ready for the opening. The
rehearsals had proceeded well, the cast enjoying rehearsals, their
confidence in the play growing.[15]

The second dress rehearsal was a grim experience. Before a small
invited audience, including the backers, Rattigan's boss at Warner
Brothers, veteran of the Aldwych farces, Ralph Lynn, and
Rattigan's mother, the performance stumbled from disaster to
disaster: 'Trevor Howard "dried" on his second line, Rex Harrison
played as though he were constipated and didn't care who knew it,
Roland Culver put in more "ers" than he had done at the reading,
Jessica Tandy was so slow she might have been on a modern
strike, Percy Walsh forgot he was playing a Frenchman and every
now and then lapsed into an Oxford accent.'[16] Albery immediately
made plans to bring in another show which was touring the
regions; Alban Limpus, one of the backers, offloaded his share in
the production to a theatrical agency, and Rattigan's own agent
wandered between members of the cast trying to sell his £500
stake for a fifth of its original value.

French went backstage and berated his cast for their appalling
performances and announced that there would be third dress
rehearsal in fifteen minutes and went in search of Rattigan. He
found the author looking dejected in the foyer. He took the news
of the third dress very badly: 'I . . . I . . . don't think I could stand
it again'.[17] Reluctantly, Rattigan was led down to the stalls and
watched the cast pull together a credible semblance of the
rehearsed play. But he was pessimistic about his play's chances.
When the curtain rose on the first night, Rattigan had all but
written off any chance of success.

In the event, the audience, led by the 'deep-throated gurgle' of
Cicely Courtneidge, laughed at the very first joke, and were soon
laughing at every gag, every piece of business.[18] Only Harold
French was concerned, feeling that the actors were rushing the
piece, cutting through laughs and mistiming cues. But when
Roland Culver, his sole gamble in the casting, entered, and took a
laugh with the right leisurely pace, the cast found the correct
rhythm. At the curtain call, the house was calling for the author,
but Rattigan was nowhere to be found. French searched the
building until

> I found him, white-tied and tailed, green-faced and dithering,
> being supported by a convenient back wall.
>
> 'They're yelling for you, go on and thank them.'
>
> 'Come with me,' he hiccuped – a child to a nannie. I relieved

the wall of its reluctant support, took him by the scruff of the neck and threw him on to the stage.[19]

Rattigan accepted the audience applause, but the stage hands had not been alerted and as he stepped forward to make a short curtain speech, the curtains swung together trapping in their folds the brightest new playwright of the West End.[20] As the cast celebrated, Bronson Albery, the man who had spent the previous evening arranging to bring a touring show to replace it, told them 'Well, it looks as though you will be here for some time'.[21]

The approval of the audience was reflected in the reviews, which were almost entirely positive. W. A. Darlington in the *Daily Telegraph* wrote that 'the gift of real lightness is a rare one in the theatre, and Terence Rattigan is a lucky young man to have it', observing that 'this is an unpretentious entertainment; but it gets just about full marks in its class'. The same theme was picked up everywhere: the *Evening Standard* called it a 'little masterpiece of frivolity' and the *Morning Post* called it 'a brilliant little comedy', while Herbert Farjeon in *The Bystander* speculated that, 'if, by any mischance, I had fallen asleep at this, I believe my own laughter would have woken me up'.

The only dissenting voice came from James Agate in the *Sunday Times*, who wrote, 'This is not a play. It is not anything. Six Marie Tempests and six Charles Hawtreys would not be able to redeem it, because there is not a crumb of redemption in it. It is not witty. It has no plot. It is almost without characterisation'. (Agate was said to have arrived after the start to and have left before the end.) Not satisfied with panning the play's first night, he spent the next eighteen months punctuating his columns with disparaging asides directed at the play. Eventually, John Gielgud wrote a letter of protest to the newspaper, urging that critics had a duty to support new writers. The same day saw the annual Gallery First Nighters' dinner and in his speech Agate attacked Gielgud and the play. Cast member, Percy Walsh, leapt to his feet in protest and had to be ushered out. The following week Agate replied to Gielgud's criticism more formally in his regular column, insisting that the kind of theatre he longed for would 'never emerge from the critical encouragement of things like *French Without Tears*'. However, he stopped attacking the play in print.[22]

The play made stars of its leading cast and a rich man of its author. It immediately began to sell out, and, as Rex Harrison recalled, 'We became a vogue, a household word, and everybody, from royalty to aristocracy to café-society, dropped in to see us'.[23] Queen Mary came to see the play in February 1937; a Paris production (with the original ending) opened in July 1937, which ran for a year; a month later, a regional tour began and in September it opened in New York. Paramount paid five thousand pounds for the film rights of a play which Rattigan had offered for £200 only two years before, and soon he was earning well in excess of £100 a week. Always delighted to live beyond his means, Rattigan was estimated to have made in excess of £23,000 from the play and to have spent or gambled it all away by the end of the play's run, in May 1939, by which time it had achieved 1,039 performances and become London's biggest theatrical hit of the 1930s.

The success of *French Without Tears* established Rattigan's reputation, but later he began to see it as a millstone. For many years, Rattigan's plays were judged against this early success: 'Whatever I did subsequently I was always described as the author of *French Without Tears*. It took me years and years actually to get the phrase removed from programme notes'.[24] The critical responses already cited indicate slightly patronising approval; The *Tatler*'s reviewer enjoyed what he called 'less of a play than an entertaining, cleverly observed sketch of youthful outlook'. Ivor Brown, writing in the *Observer*, felt that 'the play rattles along, leading nowhere in particular, but never flagging in jovial absurdity' professing that 'Mr. Rattigan has been uncommonly well served' by a company which turned his 'brief and brittle [play], with little construction and no freshness or fun' into 'the agreeable semblance of a really gay comedy'.[25]

The play was immediately revived after it closed in the West End, with productions at the Richmond Theatre, Golders Green Hippodrome, 'Q' and Embassy Theatres in the same year. There was a European ENSA tour just after the war, with members of the original cast,[26] but its first major revival was in 1949, at the Vaudeville Theatre, London, directed by Robert Flemyng who also starred as Alan, alongside Moira Lister as Diana and Clive Morton as Rogers. By this time, audiences had seen *After the Dance, Flare Path, The Winslow Boy, The Browning Version* and *Adventure Story*, and Rattigan's change of direction was evident. The condescension intensified: the *Sketch* talked of 'the virtues of this little piece'; the *Times* suggested that it was 'only a trifle . . . but it has an air of high spirits and good humour that can still be delightful'; the *Daily Herald* found it 'airy fun' and the *Daily Mail* 'a sunny, airy affair'.[27] Ironically, then, the play which had hampered Rattigan's more sombre work would itself become dismissed by this later development.

The play continued to be revived over the next fifteen years, including productions at the Croydon Grand (1950 and 1954), Camberwell Palace (1951), Brighton Theatre Royal (1956), Nottingham Playhouse (1958), and Sheffield Playhouse (1963). But as with all of Rattigan's work, the play's fortunes went into a decline during the sixties, as a new generation of playwrights held Britain's critical attention.

It was therefore surprising to some that Frank Dunlop should have chosen, in 1973, to revive *French Without Tears* at the Young Vic, a fringe theatre associated with younger audiences. It starred Ian Charleson as Brian, Andrew Robertson as Alan, Gavin Reed as Rogers and Mel Martin as Diana. While the *Daily Mail* reviewer in 1949 could begin a review with the words, 'Terence Rattigan, today one of our major playwrights . . . ', no one could do that in 1973.

And yet the production was an enormous success. Robert Cushman, in the *Observer*, wrote that 'the construction is famously adroit, and the writing bubbles. The play richly deserves its audience, which, as usual at this theatre, is predominantly young, and apparently greatly relieved at being allowed to escape from what is generally held to be good for it'. The *Sunday Times* reviewer described the play as 'one of the funniest in English literature', a view echoed by Dunlop who called it 'one of the best comedies of our epoch'.[28]

Coming soon after a revival of *While the Sun Shines* at Hampstead, the play marked an upturn in Rattigan's critical reputation, characterised by Charles Lewsen's remark in the *Times* that 'possibly the theatre of the sixties unjustly neglected a fine comic writer'. Rattigan, who went to the first night with Rex Harrison, was very moved by this reappraisal of his reputation: 'It was quite absurd. There we were with tears streaming down our faces and all around us sat the audience laughing their heads off. But the point was they were so young. Some of them could have been our grandchildren; most of them weren't even born when the play was first staged. I felt immensely grateful to all of them. We crept out mopping our eyes and feeling absolutely marvellous'.[29]

The play has been less frequently revived since then, directors favouring the later Rattigan of the forties and fifties. In 1982, Alan Strachan, who had directed a series of Coward revivals which had been instrumental in reanimating his critical profile, as well as a successful version of *The Deep Blue Sea* the year before, revived *French Without Tears* at the Greenwich Theatre. Clive Francis played Rogers, Jane Booker Diana, and Peter Woodward Alan. Although the cast were generally complimented, most reviews registered an unease with what seemed like a curiosity from a forgotten era. 'Somehow,' wrote Sheridan Morley in *Punch*, 'this curious parable of sexual frigidity and promiscuity is now showing a few hairline cracks,' and voiced the now routine claim, also alleged by Nicholas de Jongh in the *Guardian*, that Rattigan's failure to acknowledge his homosexuality gives his plays a central, structural dishonesty. At best the critics found it 'a pleasant, diverting evening' (*Time Out*), but at worst called it 'the dated grand-daddy of English sit-coms' (*City Limits*). Morley's view that 'Rattigan's comedies are now wearing a lot worse than his dramas' was widely shared.[30]

How does the play look today? John Barber, without elaborating, wrote of the Young Vic revival: 'So we were not wrong, those of us who remember *French Without Tears* as delicious and somehow something more than a mere frolic.' To contemporary eyes, the play may well be said to have dated. We are rightly inclined to take less indulgently the men's malicious discussion of womanly wiles. It is equally hard to be persuaded of Diana's fatal attractions. The play remains light, colloquially witty, but, to pursue Barber's point, is there 'something more'?

It may well be the very features that have caused recent reviewers such problems that could commend the play to us. What is particularly striking now is the misogyny of the male characters. Diana is an object of 'caddish' derision in the play, referred to a number of times as a 'bitch', and the play ends with her humiliation as Lord Heybrook evades her clutches. However, the play does not necessarily endorse this; rather it presents a subtle dramatisation of the tensions within this misogyny. And from this much of the play's comedy springs.

For even if we should wish to, it is hard fully to sympathise with these men. Part of the humour lies in the audience's awareness of how Diana works. Her flirting is utterly transparent, and we laugh at the fact that these men seem so easily taken in. Rogers has been warned that Diana will try to seduce him, but when she makes her first advance he is totally captivated:

> DIANA. . . . Tell me about yourself. Tell me about the Navy. I'm always thrilled to death by anything to do with the sea.
>
> ROGERS. Really, that's splendid. (p. 23)

Similarly, we watch Diana stringing Rogers and Kit along simultaneously, and laugh when she uses exactly the same line to both men and neither of them doubts her sincerity. These moments give us an ironic distance on events like Alan's seduction. The discrepancy between the men's description of Diana as this mysterious, seductive huntress and her really rather conspicuous technique creates a space for satirical observation of the mechanics of male attitudes to women. In Act Three, Kit's attempt to make romantic overtures to Jacqueline by talking about the weather and Alan's increasingly panicked and farcical attempts to avoid being in the same room as Diana make for an emphatic satire of male fears and anxieties.

Not simply hostile, the men betray a profound ambivalence towards Diana. One of the first things they say about her is that she is not there to learn French but to stop them learning it (p. 11). This immediately establishes a central irony that runs through the play. Most of the men have been sent by their fathers to learn French before taking their exams to enter the Diplomatic service.

Yet they all spend the play trying to avoid learning any French. Diana is immediately characterised as someone who both challenges their serious careers and yet makes possible their pleasure.

Unable to accept responsibility for their resistance to paternal authority, these men displace these desires onto Diana, disavowing any responsibility for them. Their panicked reactions to her advances are in fact fears about the instability of their own resolve, their own desires. This hypocritical move is a difficult one to sustain, and their simultaneous desire and disdain for Diana leads them to ever more violent attempts to dissociate themselves from her. Their characterisation of relations between them and her move from embarrassed allegations that she is 'rather fast' (p.12) to describing their defence against her in military terms: confronting Diana, Alan observes his petrified fellow-students and asks, 'Who is to fire the first shot of the salvo? . . . Very well, I must engage the enemy on your behalf' (p. 60).

The conflict between their desires and their fathers' instructions to work hard is depicted at Maingot's dinner table, where they attempt to present a serious face while secretly passing notes and planning their leisure time. The serious, tightly-reined image of propriety is indicated through their clothing; while Diana seems entirely comfortable with her body (often making entrances semi-naked), the men wear shapeless clothes, or formal jackets that hide their bodies. Rogers is the clearest example of this neurotically strait-laced, tight-lipped, ship-shape orderliness. Part of Alan's astonishment at Kit's decision to take an early dip is no doubt connected with this unmanly exposure of his body; and when Jacqueline tells Diana that Kit has gone upstairs to put some clothes on, she remarks, 'isn't that like him' (p. 21).

The association between bodily containment and controlling one's desires is revealed further by a series of fantasies of the disastrous effects of love, which threatens to tear their very bodies apart: Kit accuses Diana of having given him pneumonia after she persuades him to go for an early morning dip: 'But I don't mind,' he adds. 'You could tear me up in little pieces and trample on them, and I'd still love you' (p. 19). Alan's description of Diana's seduction technique is revealingly couched in metaphors drawn from the blood sports of fishing and stag hunting (pp. 35-36); and when he discovers that Diana may be in love with him, his response is sheer terror: 'I'm frightened. I'm really frightened. . . . I shall fall. Oh, God! I know it, I shall fall . . . You don't realise the appalling danger I'm in' (p. 61).

To avoid the projected dangers of Diana, the men constantly retreat into apparently non-sexual environments; some of the time they behave like schoolchildren, passing notes in class, inventing outlandish excuses for failing to submit essays, and are referred to as 'boys' (e.g., p. 21). Brian, in his visits to prostitutes, tries to reduce his dealings with women to simple economic contracts, for which Alan admires him. But mainly they find refuge in manly comradeship. At the end of the first scene of Act Two, Alan tells Rogers about his novel. It concerns two conscientious objectors who emigrate so as to avoid having to fight in a war, but soon find themselves fighting over a woman. Eventually, they decide to abandon the woman and their principles and go off to war together (p. 41).

This renunciation of women and celebration of brotherly companionship is not altogether without its problems. The men surround the second main female character, Jacqueline, with another series of strange disavowals. Their friendliness towards her would seem to bear out the passage from La Bruyère that Kit so incompetently and pessimistically translates ('Friendship can exist between people of different sexes, *quite exempt from all grossness*,' p. 27). But the only way these men can sustain a friendship with her is by treating her as 'one of the boys'. They all call her 'Jack', and Kit admits to her, 'I'll tell you this, Jack. I like you so much that it's sometimes quite an effort to remember that you're a woman at all' (p. 33).

But this strategy causes them problems; Jack/Jacqueline crosses the boundary they try rigorously to police between honest male friendship and dangerous sexual desires. When Alan informs Kit that she is in love with him, he is strangely disconcerted: 'Love and Jack. They just don't seem to connect. I'm frightfully fond of her, but somehow – I don't know – I mean you couldn't kiss her or make love to her' (p. 62). And at one point, trying to attract Kit, Jacqueline has her hair cut in imitation of Diana. He admits that this makes her look 'alluring' and laughs. Pressed for an opinion, he retorts rudely and leaves the room (p. 28). What perhaps disturbs Kit is that their carefully protected male cameraderie may not be quite as non-sexual as they had hoped.

Through such devices, the play brilliantly anatomises the sexual dynamics of all-male environments. The men's tortuous attempts to preserve their bodily and sexual integrity is frequently defeated by shrewd ambiguities and tensions. Alan's description of his ideal woman is that she should not be a 'cow' (further abuse of Diana), and also that 'she will be able to converse freely and intelligently with me on all subjects – Politics – Philosophy – Religion – Thirdly, she will have all the masculine virtues and none of the feminine vices. Fourthly, she will be physically unattractive enough to keep her faithful to me, and attractive enough to make me desire her' (p. 62). Especially given Alan's, Kit's and Rogers's determination that proper masculine behaviour involves the inflexible application of rationality, this woman who has no power to set man against man begins rather to resemble a man herself.

Throughout the play, their staunchly masculine comradeship is marked by traces of homoeroticism. Much of the time this means the adoption of a tone of camp *badinage*: in the first moments of the play we discover that the men refer to each other as 'Babe', 'my dear', 'child' and 'ducky' (p. 5), and a sweetly effete stage direction as Alan 'taps Kenneth on the head with a brioche' (p. 6).

The most striking sequence follows these men on the night of the Costume Ball. Under the influence of the festivities, these otherwise unacknowledged forces surface to hilarious effect. Mikhail Bakhtin has written of a history of popular celebration in which hierarchy and order is replaced by a riotous confusion, blurring of boundaries, excess, reversal and laughter. In carnival, he writes, 'things are tested and re-evaluated in the dimensions of laughter . . . it liberates objects from the snares of false seriousness, from illusions and sublimations inspired by fear' adding, as just one example, 'men are transvested as women and vice versa'.[31]

The mini-carnival of Le Quartorze, Bastille Day, sees the men throw off their tightly-reined seriousness. The shabby clothes are replaced with a new flamboyance: Kit is wearing the costume of a Greek Evzone, the most notable feature of which is a skirt, beneath which, comically, sock-suspenders can be seen; adopting Rogers's proper dress, Kenneth wears a sailor suit (the ability of which to emphasise the body is much admired in certain theatrical quarters); and even the ferocious patriarch, Maingot, wears a kilt.

These costumes have peculiar effects on their wearers' masculinity; Kit describes himself as looking like an 'inebriated danseuse' (p. 47), and Maingot confusing it with a ceilidh, announces his intention to perform a 'can-can' (p. 48). The serious dispute between Rogers and Kit over Diana is rendered impossible by the costume:

> ROGERS. (*Collapsing, doubled up with laughter, into a chair.*) You look so damned funny in that get up.
>
> KIT. (*Looking down at his legs, and beginning to giggle.*) A little eccentric, I admit.
>
> ROGERS. Like a bedraggled old fairy queen.
>
> KIT. I'll go and change.
>
> ROGERS. (*Becoming serious.*) No, don't. If you do I'll have to fight you. I can't when you're looking like that, and if you go on looking like that it'll save us from making idiots of ourselves. (p. 50)

So Rogers, the man who felt that fighting for honour is proof of manhood (p. 41), now finds that fighting makes you look ridiculous.

Their attempts to keep their 'animal passions' at bay by reasoning with each other (p. 51) soon evaporate, and, as if cued by the skirt, their comradeship becomes inflected with a camp register that recalls Gwendolen and Cecily from *The Importance of Being Earnest*.

> KIT. . . . I say, I may call you Bill, mayn't I?
>
> ROGERS. Oh, my dear Kit. (p. 53)

When Alan appears, they describe their new-found friendship almost as if declaring their engagement, and he is soon caught up in the festivity:

> KIT. Don't call him the Commander, Alan. His name is Bill.
>
> ALAN. Bill?
>
> KIT. Yes, Bill. He's one of the best fellows in the world.
>
> ROGERS. We're going to get drunk together, aren't we, Kit?
>
> ALAN. Kit?
>
> KIT. Screaming drunk, Bill.
>
> ALAN. (*Dashing to the door*.) I won't be a minute. (p. 54)

The playful homoeroticism of this sequence is accentuated in the following scene. As the curtain rises, in a muted take on a post-coital tableau, the men are discovered lounging sleepily on the set, smoking. When Kit threatens to break up this masculine bond, Rogers flirtatiously makes a grab for him: 'Very well. I have no option but to ask you for your skirt . . . I've been longing to get my hands on that damn thing all the evening' (p. 59). The three men tumble to the floor. Diana's entrance provokes a witty re-framing that makes it quite clear 'what this looks like', a speculation strengthened from within the play by Rogers citing Freud to the effect that love – and possibly friendship – is 'sublimated sex' (p. 56). Rattigan's decision to change Lord Heybrook to a young boy was wise, since having the men laugh complicitly with a blonde queen would have articulated too clearly an unmentionable aspect of their sexual victory.

The inability of these men to find refuge from their own desires is perceived by the men as their tragedy, but in fact provides the comedy of the play. While men like Kit and Brian are distracted from their work by women, Alan's conflict, as was Rattigan's at Wimereux, is between work and his own writing. Alan, the confirmed bachelor, refers to his rejected novel as having 'come home to father', implying a non-sexual surrogate for his sexuality

(p. 40). But when Diana threatens his celibate integrity, he has to make a choice between her and his writing, and forces Diana to make the decision for him. At the end of the play, Alan is leaving to pursue his writing career, but Diana sets off to pursue him to England. Nowhere is safe for the man fleeing his own desires: 'Stop laughing, you idiots,' he cries. 'It isn't funny. It's a bloody tragedy' (p. 80).

Now plainly *French Without Tears* is not a Strindbergian tragedy of sexual paranoia. But it deals with these themes through the medium of comedy, and, as Michael Billington observed of the Young Vic revival, 'mocks certain durable aspects of the English character' in ways that would be explored further in plays like *The Browning Version*, *The Deep Blue Sea* and *Separate Tables*. Rattigan had considerable experience of all-male environments, and we may speculate that setting the atmosphere of Harrow against the rather different gay male set that he mixed with when visiting Gielgud and John Perry at their home in Henley-on-Thames gave Rattigan the lever he needed to develop an ironic distance on some of the more exotic alibis of heterosexual male behaviour.

Aside from theatrical revivals, *French Without Tears* enjoyed a successful film production in 1939, directed by Anthony Asquith, a radio revival in 1957 and a television production as part of BBC1's 'Play of the Month' series in 1976.

Perhaps the most curious, certainly the least successful, version of the play was as a musical, entitled *Joie de Vivre* (the play's very first title), which premièred in 1960 at the Queen's Theatre, London. Unlike the adaptation of his play, *The Sleeping Prince*, turned into a musical by Noël Coward as *The Girl Who Came to Supper* in 1962, Rattigan wrote the book himself, collaborating with the composer Robert Stolz, and his Oxford contemporary, the lyricist Paul Dehn. It starred Donald Sinden as Brian, Barry Ingham as Alan, Joanne Rigby as Diana, and Joan Heal as Chi-Chi, and featured a large chorus of dancers, including Lindsay Kemp.

It was relocated to the Île de Tourterelles, off the French mainland, rewritten to include a subplot about the island being cursed by the spirit of Venus, and brought the off-stage Chi-Chi on-stage, filling the *soubrette* role of musical theatre convention. In place of the simplicity of the original conception, Rattigan used the resources of a large theatre and a revolving stage to include scenes in the ruined temple of Venus and on the boat leaving for England. The play was also updated by some rather feeble references to the nuclear threat and, even more unwisely, given the direction of the theatrical tide, some sniping jokes at the expense of the Royal Court dramatists. Brian sings a song in which he confesses that 'I ought to strip myself / So as to whip myself / Into a sharp, short

Royal Court rage. / I ought to so-und off / Because I'm bro-wned off / With the errors and the terrors of an angry modern stage' but cannot because 'I'm sorry – But I'm Happy'.[32] Even worse, Rattigan abandoned the witty ambiguities of the original to endorse the mystical powers of Venus, who intervenes on Diana's behalf, and occasionally comments clumsily on the action with rolls of thunder and mysterious, echoing laughter.

Parts of this musical *are* wittily done. In an extra scene added on the end, Chi-Chi has accumulated enough money to travel to London to ply her trade there, and Alan is racing for the boat, hoping Diana will miss it. He hurls himself on board and the boat moves off; just at that moment, Diana appears over the edge of the boat, lifted by two sailors from a launch, looking like Venus rising from the sea. The most successful musical number is sung by Chi-Chi who, in broken English, imagines the fun she will have in London exploring 'Le West End'. A series of witty idealisations of London include delighted speculations about the theatre, as she looks forward to 'Ze 'Bravo!" and ze 'Boo!"'.[33]

Sadly for Rattigan, *Joie de Vivre* received very much more Boo than Bravo. For the first time in his career, a play was actually booed at the curtain. Written in a pre-war musical style, it was unfavourably compared to a series of successful American imports, and the critics were scathing, describing it as 'schoolboyish' (*Observer*), 'a bore' (*Guardian*), 'the most misconceived, miscast, mis-managed show of 1960' (*Sunday Despatch*), and 'the saddest evening I have spent in the theatre this year' (*Daily Telegraph*). Rattigan was stoical, driving to Ascot the next day, where, he said, 'nobody mentioned the play at all. They all behaved as though my mother had just died. Most peculiar'.[34] The play closed after just four performances.

But *French Without Tears* was a triumph for Rattigan. Although, he would later resent his work being judged against this play, the play retains the exuberance and energy of its youthful origin. The play ran during a time of escalating European crisis, and although the play refers occasionally to Hitler's rise in Germany, and Alan's novel is a partial defence of Rattigan's own pacifism, the political context of the play is kept very much in the wings. Rattigan would soon take a very different direction, his work becoming increasingly complicated by social questions, his tone darkened by explorations in the more desolate fields of love and desire.

DAN REBELLATO

Notes.

1. Michael Darlow and Gillian Hodson. *Terence Rattigan: The Man and His Work*. London and New York: Quartet Books, 1979, pp. 47-48. Rattigan's own recollections may be found in Philip Oakes. 'Comédie Anglaise.' *Radio Times*. (13 May 1976), p. 60.

2. Philip Oakes, *ibid.*, pp. 60-61.

3. Darlow and Hodson, *op. cit.*, p. 72.

4. Anthony Powell. *To Keep the Ball Rolling – Memoirs Volume Three: Faces in My Time*. London: Heinemann, 1980, p. 39.

5. Darlow and Hodson, *op. cit.*, p. 75.

6. Anthony Powell, *op. cit.*, pp. 39-40.

7. Harold French. *I Thought I Never Could*. London: Secker & Warburg, 1973, p. 151.

8. *Ibid.*, p. 154.

9. Roland Culver. *Not Quite a Gentleman*. London: William Kimber, 1979, p. 86; Rex Harrison. *A Damned Serious Business*. London: Bantam, 1990, p. 55. See also Nicholas Wapshott. *Rex Harrison: A Biography*. London: Chatto & Windus, 1991, p. 49.

10. Harold French, *op. cit.*, p. 155.

11. Terence Rattigan. Foreword. in Harold French, *op. cit.*, pp. vii-viii.

12. Alexander Walker. *Fatal Charm: The Life of Rex Harrison*. London: Weidenfeld and Nicolson, 1992, p. 67. See also Roy Moseley and Philip and Martin Masheter. *Rex Harrison: The First Biography*. London: New English Library, 1987, p. 34, and Nicholas Wapshott. *op. cit.*, p. 50.

13. Terence Rattigan. *French Without Tears*. Typescript. Lord Chamberlain Play Collection: 1936/44. [British Library]. pp. III, 37-38.

14. Rattigan, quoted in Harold French, *op. cit.*, pp. 156-8.

15. Roland Culver, *op. cit.*, p. 86.

16. Harold French, *op. cit.*, p. 158.

17. *Ibid.*, p. 160.

18. *Ibid.*, p. 161.

19. *Ibid.*, p. 162.

20. B. A. Young. *The Rattigan Version: Sir Terence Rattigan and the Theatre of Character*. Hamish Hamilton: London, 1986, p. 25.

21. Roland Culver, *op. cit.*, p. 87.

22. B. A. Young, *op. cit.*, p. 26; and Darlow and Hodson, *op. cit.*, pp. 88-89. Reviews quoted from B. A. Young, p. 25, or from the Production File for *French Without Tears*. Criterion Theatre. 6 November 1936, in the Theatre Museum, London.

23. Rex Harrison, *op. cit.*, p. 57.

24. Philip Oakes, *op. cit.*, p. 60.

25. See note 22.

26. Rex Harrison. *Rex: An Autobiography*, London: Macmillan, 1974, p. 82; Culver, *op. cit.*, p. 106; Moseley and Masheter, *op. cit.*, p. 79. The production starred Harrison, Culver and Walsh, with Anna Neagle taking Hammond's rôle. It toured Holland, Belgium and France, playing to troops still stationed in Europe.

27. Reviews quoted from the Production File for *French Without Tears*. Vaudeville Theatre. 15 June 1949, in the Theatre Museum, London.

28. Reviews quoted from the Production File for *French Without Tears*. Young Vic Theatre. 27 July 1973, in the Theatre Museum, London.

29. Philip Oakes, *op. cit.*, p. 60.

30. Reviews can be found in *London Theatre Record*. ii, 25/26 (2-31 December 1982), pp. 693-694.

31. Mikhail Bakhtin. *Rabelais and His World*. Translated by Helene Iswolsky. Bloomington: Indiana University Press, 1984, pp. 376, 411.

32. Terence Rattigan and Paul Dehn. *Joie de Vivre*. Typescript. Lord Chamberlain Play Collection: 1960/15. [British Library.] INSERT, p. II, 34.

33. *Ibid.,* p. II, 31.

34. Reviews and interview quoted from the Production File for *Joie de Vivre*. Queen's Theatre. 14 July 1960, in the Theatre Museum, London.

List of Rattigan's Produced Plays

TITLE	BRITISH PREMIERE	NEW YORK PREMIERE
First Episode (with Philip Heimann)	Q Theatre, Kew, 11 Sept 1933 (transferred to Comedy Theatre, 26 Jan 1934)	Ritz Theatre, 17 Sept 1934
French Without Tears	Criterion Theatre, 6 Nov 1936	Henry Miller Theatre, 28 Sept 1937
After the Dance	St James's Theatre, 21 June 1939	
Follow My Leader (with Anthony Maurice, alias Tony Goldschmidt)	Apollo Theatre, 16 Jan 1940	
Grey Farm (with Hector Bolitho)		Hudson Theatre, 3 May 1940
Flare Path	Apollo Theatre, 13 Aug 1932	Henry Miller Theatre, 23 Dec 1942
While the Sun Shines	Globe Theatre, 24 Dec 1943	Lyceum Theatre, 19 Sept 1944
Love in Idleness	Lyric Theatre, 20 Dec 1944	Empire Theatre (as *O Mistress Mine*), 23 Jan 1946
The Winslow Boy	Lyric Theatre, 23 May 1946	Empire Theatre, 29 Oct 1947
Playbill (*The Browning Version* and *Harlequinade*)	Phoenix Theatre, 8 Sept 1948	Coronet Theatre, 12 Oct 1949
Adventure Story	St James's Theatre, 17 March 1949	
A Tale of Two Cities (from Charles Dickens, with John Gielgud)	St Brendan's College Dramatic Society, Clifton, 23 Jan 1950	
Who is Sylvia?	Criterion Theatre, 24 Oct 1950	
Final Test (TV)	BBC TV, 29 July 1951	

The Deep Blue Sea	Duchess Theatre, 6 Mar 1952	Morosco Theatre, 5 Nov 1952
The Sleeping Prince	Phoenix Theatre, 5 Nov 1953	Coronet Theatre, 1 Nov 1956
Seperate Tables (*The Table by the Window* and *Table Number Seven*)	St James's Theatre, 22 Sept 1954	Music Box Theatre, 25 Oct 1956
Variation on a Theme	Globe Theatre, 8 May 1958	
Ross Theatre	Theatre Royal Haymarket 12 May 1960	Eugene O'Neill 26 Dec 1961
Joie de Vivre (with Robert Stolz and Paul Dehn)	Queen's Theatre, 14 July 1960	
Heart to Heart (TV)	BBC TV, 6 Dec 1962	
Man and Boy	Queen's Theatre, 4 Sept 1963	Brooks Atkinson Theatre, 12 Nov 1963
Ninety Years On (TV)	BBC TV, 29 Nov 1964	
Nelson – A Portrait in Miniature (TV)	Associated Television, 21 Mar 1966	
All On Her Own (TV) (adapted for the stage as *Duologue*)	BBC 2, 25 Sept 1968	
A Bequest to the Nation	Theatre Royal Haymarket 23 Sept 1970	
High Summer (TV)	Thames TV, 12 Sept 1972	
In Praise of Love (*After Lydia* and *Before Dawn*)	Duchess Theatre, 27 Sept 1973	Morosco Theatre, 10 Dec 1974
Cause Célèbre (radio)	BBC Radio 4, 27 Oct 1975	
Duologue	King's Head Theatre, 21 Feb 1976	
Cause Célèbre (stage)	Her Majesty's Theatre, 4 July 1977	
Less Than Kind	Jermyn Street Theatre, 20 January 2011	

This edition of *French Without Tears* was published alongside the revival at the Orange Tree Theatre, Richmond, from 8 October 2015, with the following cast:

KENNETH LAKE	Patrick McNamee
BRIAN CURTIS	Tom Hanson
HON. ALAN HOWARD	Alex Bhat
MARIANNE	Laila Alj
MONSIEUR MAINGOT	David Whitworth
LT.-CMDR. ROGERS	William Belchambers
DIANA LAKE	Genevieve Gaunt
KIT NEILAN	Joe Eyre
JACQUELINE MAINGOT	Sarah Winter

Director	Paul Miller
Designer	Simon Daw
Lighting Designer	Mark Doubleday
Composer	David Shrubsole
Costume Supervisor	Holly Rose Henshaw
Fight Director	Terry King
Casting Consultant	Ellie Collyer-Bristow

French Without Tears was first produced at the Criterion Theatre, London, on 6 November 1936, with the following cast:

KENNETH LAKE	Trevor Howard
BRIAN CURTIS	Guy Middleton
HON. ALAN HOWARD	Rex Harrison
MARIANNE	Yvonne Andre
MONSIEUR MAINGOT	Percy Walsh
LT.-CMDR. ROGERS	Roland Culver
DIANA LAKE	Kay Hammond
KIT NEILAN	Robert Flemyng
JACQUELINE MAINGOT	Jessica Tandy
LORD HEYBROOK	William Dear
Director	Harold French

FRENCH WITHOUT TEARS

Characters

KENNETH LAKE
BRIAN CURTIS
HON. ALAN HOWARD
MARIANNE
MONSIEUR MAINGOT
LT.-CMDR. ROGERS
DIANA LAKE
KIT NEILAN
JACQUELINE MAINGOT
LORD HEYBROOK

Act One	July 1st. Morning
Act Two, Scene One	July 14th. Afternoon
Act Two, Scene Two	The same evening
Act Three, Scene One	Later the same night
Act Three, Scene Two	The following morning

The action passes in the living-room at 'Miramar', a villa in a small seaside town on the west coast of France.

Act One

Scene: The living-room at 'Miramar', a villa in a small seaside town on the west coast of France.

Time: July 1st, about 9 a.m.

The room is rather bare of furniture. There is a large, plain table in the centre, surrounded by eight kitchen chairs. There are two dilapidated armchairs against the back wall. The wallpaper is grey and dirty-looking.

On the left, two French windows open out on to a small garden. They are open at the moment, and the sun is streaming through. There is a door back right leading into the hall, and another down-stage right leading into the kitchen.

The table is laid for breakfast, with an enormous coffee-pot in the middle and a quantity of rolls.

As the curtain rises KENNETH *is discovered sitting at the table. He is about twenty, good-looking in a rather vacuous way. At the moment he is engaged in writing in a notebook with one hand, while with the other he is nibbling a roll. A dictionary lies open before him.*

There is the sound of someone heavily descending the stairs. The door at the back opens and BRIAN *comes in. He is older than* KENNETH, *about twenty-three or twenty-four, large, thick-set, and red-faced. He wears an incredibly dirty pair of grey flannel trousers, a battered brown tweed coat, and a white sweater.*

BRIAN. Morning, Babe.

> KENNETH *doesn't look up.* BRIAN *goes to the table, picks up a letter, and opens it.*

KENNETH. (*Looking musingly ahead.*) She has ideas above her station.

BRIAN. What's that?

KENNETH. How would you say that in French?

BRIAN. What?

KENNETH. She has ideas above her station.

BRIAN. She has ideas above her station. She has ideas . . .

He stuffs his letter in his pocket and goes to kitchen door calling.

Marianne!

VOICE. (*From the kitchen.*) Oui, Monsieur?

BRIAN. (*With an appalling accent.*) Deux oeufs, s'il vous plaît.

VOICE. (*Off.*) Bien, Monsieur.

BRIAN. Avec un petit peu de jambon.

VOICE. (*Off.*) Oui, Monsieur. Des oeufs brouillés, n'est-ce pas?

BRIAN. Brouillés? Ah, oui, brouillés. (*He closes the door.*) I'm getting pretty hot at this stuff, don't you think? You know, nowadays it's quite an effort for me to go back to English.

KENNETH. If you're so hot, you'd better tell me how to say she has ideas above her station.

BRIAN. Oh, yes, I forgot. It's fairly easy, old boy. Elle a des idées au-dessus de sa gare.

KENNETH. You can't do it like that. You can't say au-dessus de sa gare. It isn't that sort of station.

BRIAN. (*Pouring himself out a cup of coffee.*) Well, don't ask me.

KENNETH. I thought you were so hot at French.

BRIAN. Well, as a matter of fact, that wasn't strictly the truth. Now if a Frenchman asked me where the pen of his aunt was, the chances are I could give him a pretty snappy come-back and tell him it was in the pocket of the gardener.

KENNETH. Yes, but that doesn't help me much.

BRIAN. Sorry, old boy.

KENNETH. I suppose I'd better just do it literally. Maingot'll throw a fit.

BRIAN. That doesn't bother you, does it?

KENNETH. You're not going into the diplomatic. He doesn't really get worked up about you.

BRIAN. Well, I don't know about that. The whole of his beard came off yesterday when I was having my lesson.

KENNETH. No, but he doesn't really mind. It's absolute physical agony to him when I do something wrong. He knows as well as I do that I haven't got one chance in a thousand of getting in.

BRIAN. (*Cheerfully.*) Don't say that, old boy. You're breaking my heart.

KENNETH. (*Gloomily.*) Yes, but it's true. (*He starts to write again.*)

BRIAN. As a matter of fact, Alan told me you had a pretty good chance.

KENNETH. (*Looking up, pleased.*) Did he really?

BRIAN *nods.*

BRIAN. He ought to know, oughtn't he? Isn't he Maingot's red-hot tip for the diplomatic stakes?

KENNETH. If he was keener about getting in he'd walk it. He will anyway, I should think.

BRIAN. I think I'll make a book on the result this year. I'll lay evens on Alan – a class colt with a nice free action; will win if he can get the distance.

KENNETH. What about me?

BRIAN. I'll lay you threes about yourself.

KENNETH. Threes? More like twenties.

BRIAN. Oh, I don't know. Nice-looking colt – good stayer. Bit of a dog from the starting-gate, perhaps. Say seven to two, then.

Enter ALAN *through the door at the back. He is about twenty-three, dark and saturnine. He wears carefully creased grey flannel trousers and a German 'sport jacket'.*

Morning, Alan. We were just talking about you.

ALAN. Good morning, Brian. Good morning, Babe. (*He looks at his place at the head of the table.*) Not one blood-stained letter. What were you saying about me?

BRIAN. I'm making a book on the diplomatic stakes. I'm laying evens about you.

ALAN. (*Sitting down.*) That's not very generous.

BRIAN. Hell, you're the favourite.

ALAN. What about the startling rumours that the favourite may be scratched.

KENNETH. (*Looking up quickly.*) Why, have they accepted your novel?

ALAN. Do I look as if they'd accepted my novel?

BRIAN. I don't know how you do look when they accept your novels.

ALAN. I hope, my dear Brian, that one day you'll have a chance of finding out.

KENNETH. Well, what's this talk about your scratching?

ALAN. Perhaps just to give you a better chance, ducky.

BRIAN. You're not serious about it though, old boy?

ALAN. Probably not.

KENNETH. But you must be mad, Alan. I mean even if you do want to write you could still do it in the diplomatic. Honestly, it seems quite crazy –

ALAN. You're giving a tolerably good imitation of my father.

BRIAN. What does His Excellency have to say about the idea, by the way?

ALAN. His Excellency says that he doesn't mind me choosing my own career a bit, provided always it's the one he's chosen for me.

BRIAN. Broad-minded, eh?

ALAN. That's right. Always sees two sides to every question – his own, which is the right one; and anyone else's, which is the wrong one.

KENNETH. But seriously, Alan, you can't really be thinking –

ALAN. Oh, stop it, child, for God's sake. I didn't say I was going to scratch.

KENNETH. You said you were thinking of it.

ALAN. Well, you know that. I'm always thinking of it. I very rarely think of anything else. But I won't do it, so don't worry your dear little head about it.

He taps KENNETH *on the head with a brioche.* KENNETH *sulkily returns to his work.*

Enter MARIANNE, *the maid, with a plate of scrambled eggs and bacon, placing them in front of* BRIAN.

BRIAN. Ah, mes oeufs, as I live.

MARIANNE. (*To* ALAN.) Monsieur le Commandant, va-t-il aussi prendre des oeufs avec son déjeuner, Monsieur?

BRIAN. Oh, well – er – (*To* ALAN.) She's talking to you, old boy.

ALAN. Je ne sais rien des habitudes de Monsieur le Commandant, Marianne.

MARIANNE. Bien, Monsieur. Alors voulez-vous lui demander s'il les veut, Monsieur, lorsqu'il descend?

ALAN. Bien.

Exit MARIANNE.

BRIAN. What did she want?

ALAN. She wanted to know if the Commander took eggs with his breakfast.

BRIAN. I meant to ask you. Did you see him when he arrived last night?

ALAN. Yes, I went to the station with Maingot to meet him.

BRIAN. What's he like?

ALAN. Very naval commander.

BRIAN. Yes, old boy, but what's that?

ALAN. You know. Carries with him the salty tang of the sea wherever he goes.

BRIAN. Pity he's carried it here. Paucot-sur-mer could do without any more salty tang than it's got already. Has he a rolling gait?

ALAN. He was sober when he arrived.

BRIAN. No, old boy, drunk or sober, all sailors have a rolling gait.

MONSIEUR MAINGOT comes in hurriedly through the door at the back. He is about sixty, with a ferocious face and a white beard.

MAINGOT. Bonjour – Bonjour – Bonjour!

All three rise. He shakes hands with each in turn, then sits down at the head of the table right at the opposite end to the three boys.

Mon Dieu, que je suis en retard ce matin! (*He opens a letter.*)

BRIAN. (*Speaking in a whisper to* ALAN.) What's he like, though, really?

ALAN. (*Also in a whisper.*) Pretty hellish, I thought.

BRIAN. Po-faced, I suppose?

MAINGOT. (*Roaring into his letter.*) Français! Voulez-vous parlez français, Messieurs, s'il vous plaît.

Pause.

(*Looking up from his letter.*) Qu'est-ce que c'est que ça, po-faced?

ALAN. Nous disions que Monsieur le Commandant avait une figure de vase de nuit, Monsieur.

MAINGOT. Ah! Mais c'est pas vrai.

ALAN. Nous exaggérons un peu.

MAINGOT. Je crois bien.

He returns to his letters.

KENNETH *surreptitiously pushes his notebook towards* ALAN, *pointing at a certain sentence.* ALAN *reads it and shakes his head violently.* KENNETH *looks pleadingly at him.* ALAN *considers and is about to speak when* MAINGOT *looks up.*

Dîtes-moi, est-ce-que vous connaissez un Lord Heybrook? (*Looking at letter.*)

ALAN. Non, Monsieur.

MAINGOT. Il voudrait venir le quinze Juillet.

ALAN. (*To* BRIAN.) Do you know him?

BRIAN. Lord Heybrook? No, old boy. (*Confidentially.*) As a matter of fact, I knew a peer once, but he died. What about Lord Heybrook, anyway?

ALAN. He's coming here on the fifteenth.

MAINGOT. (*Roaring.*) Français, Messieurs – français!

Pause.

MAINGOT *takes up the* Matin *and begins to read.* KENNETH *again pushes his notebook towards* ALAN, *and* ALAN *again is about to speak.*

(*Roaring.*) Ah! Ce Hitler! (*Throwing paper on floor.*) Quel phenomène!

ALAN *closes his mouth and* KENNETH *pulls his notebook back quickly.*

(*To* BRIAN.) Aha, Monsieur Curtis, vous étiez saôul au Casino hier soir, n'est-ce pas?

BRIAN. (*Puzzled.*) Saôul?

ALAN. Drunk.

BRIAN. Oh, non, Monsieur. Pas ça. Un peu huilé, peut-être.

COMMANDER ROGERS *comes in. He is about thirty-five, dark, small, very neat, rather solemn. All get up.*

MAINGOT. Ah, Bonjour, Monsieur le Commandant, et comment allez-vous? J'espère que vous avez bien dormi? Ah, pardon! (*Introducing the others.*) Monsieur Curtis – Monsieur le Commandant Rogers. Monsieur Lake – Monsieur le Commandant Rogers. Monsieur Howard – vous connaissez déjà.

BRIAN *and* KENNETH *shake hands.*

ALAN. Bonjour! (*To* ROGERS.)

ROGERS. Yes, we met last night. (*Indicating a chair.*) Shall I sit here?

ALAN. That's Kit Neilan's place, as a matter of fact. I think this is your place. (*He shows a place next to* MAINGOT.)

MAINGOT. (*Rising.*) Ah! Pardon, Monsieur le Commandant. Voilà votre place. Asseyez-vous donc et soyez à votre aise.

ROGERS. Thanks. (*He sits.*)

ALAN. I've been told to ask you if you like eggs with your breakfast.

MAINGOT. Oui, Monsieur. Mais voulez-vous parlez français, s'il vous plaît.

ROGERS. (*Smiling apologetically.*) I'm afraid I don't speak your lingo at all, you know.

MAINGOT. Lingo? Ah, oui, langue. C'est ça. Mais il faut essayer. You – must – try.

ROGERS. (*Turning to* MAINGOT, *then to* ALAN.) Oui – Non.

ALAN. What?

MAINGOT. Pardon?

ROGERS. Oui, je ne – want any eggs.

ALAN. Right, I'll tell Marianne. (*He gets up and goes into the kitchen.*)

MAINGOT. (*To* ROGERS.) Il faut dire: Je ne veux pas des oeufs pour mon petit déjeuner.

ROGERS *smiles vaguely.* MAINGOT *laughs.*

Ça viendra, ça viendra.

Re-enter ALAN.

BRIAN. I say, sir, did you have a good crossing?

ROGERS. Pretty bad, as a matter of fact. Still, that didn't worry me.

BRIAN. You're a good sailor?

ALAN *laughs.*

Oh, of course you would be. I mean you are, aren't you?

MAINGOT *gets up.*

MAINGOT. Eh, bien. Par qui vais-je commencer?

KENNETH. Moi, Monsieur.

MAINGOT. *Par* Moi. (*Rising.*) Alors, allons dans le jardin. (*Bowing.*) Messieurs!

He goes out into garden, followed by KENNETH.

ALAN. Poor Babe! He's going to be slaughtered.

ROGERS. Really. Why?

ALAN. (*Shaking his head sadly.*) Elle a des idées au-dessus de sa gare.

ROGERS. What does that mean?

ALAN. It doesn't mean she has ideas above her station.

ROGERS. The Professor is pretty strict, I suppose.

ALAN. Where work is concerned, he's a sadist.

ROGERS. I'm glad to hear it. I want to learn as much French as I can, and I'm starting from scratch, you know.

BRIAN. Are you learning it for any special reason, sir?

ROGERS. Yes. Interpretership exam in seven months' time.

ALAN. If you stay here for seven months you'll either be dead or a Frenchman.

ROGERS. How long have you been here?

ALAN. On and off for a year, but then, I have a way of preserving my nationality. I wear a special charm. (*He indicates his German coat.*)

ROGERS. Are you very pro-German, then?

BRIAN. He only wears that coat to annoy Maingot.

ROGERS. Oh, I see. What do you wear in Germany?

ALAN. A beret usually. Sabots are too uncomfortable.

ROGERS *laughs politely. There is a pause, broken suddenly by a roar coming from the garden.*

MAINGOT. (*Off.*) Aha, ça c'est formidable! Qu'est ce que vous me fichez là donc? 'Elle a des idées au-dessus de sa gare'. Idiot! Idiot! Idiot!

The noise subsides. ALAN *shakes his head.*

ALAN. Poor Babe. But he had it coming to him.

BRIAN. The Babe was having the horrors this morning before you came down. He said he hadn't one chance in a thousand of getting in.

ALAN. He hasn't.

ROGERS. Of getting in what?

ALAN. The diplomatic.

ROGERS. Oh, I suppose you're all budding diplomats?

BRIAN. All except me. I'm learning French for – er – commercial reasons.

ALAN. He's learnt a lot already. He can say 'How much?' in French, and you know how valuable that phrase is in the world of – er – commerce.

BRIAN. (*Laughing heartily*.) Yes, old boy, and that's not all. I can say, 'Five francs? Do you think I'm made of money?'

ALAN. (*Laughing too*.) 'Cinq francs? Crois-tu que je sois construit d'argent?'

They both suddenly become aware that ROGERS *isn't laughing. They stop and there is rather an awkward pause.* ALAN *and* BRIAN *exchange a brief glance.* BRIAN *silently frames the word 'Po-faced' in his mouth.*

ROGERS. (*With a wooden face*.) Who else is staying here at the moment?

ALAN. There's only Kit Neilan, I think, that you haven't met.

ROGERS. Oh! Is he going into the diplomatic, too?

ALAN. Yes. (*To* BRIAN.) By the way, Brian, what odds did you lay against Kit in your book?

BRIAN. I didn't, but I should think five to two against would about meet the case.

ALAN. I don't know. The odds must have lengthened considerably these last few weeks.

BRIAN. Why? Oh, you mean Diana. I say, old boy, I hadn't thought of that. You don't think there's a chance of a well-fancied colt being withdrawn before the big contest?

ALAN. No. She won't marry him. That is, not until she's exhausted other possibilities.

ROGERS. Er – who is this girl?

BRIAN. Diana? She's Babe's – Kenneth Lake's sister. She's staying here.

ROGERS. Oh! Is she learning French, too?

BRIAN. No. She just stops us from learning it. No, she's staying here because her people live in India and she's got nowhere else to go.

ROGERS. Pretty dull for her here, I should think.

ALAN. That girl wouldn't find it dull on a desert island.

BRIAN. Unless it *was* deserted.

ALAN. True. But one feels somehow it wouldn't be deserted long if she were on it.

ROGERS. What do you mean by that?

ALAN. I've no idea. She's a nice girl. You'll love her.

BRIAN *hides a smile*.

At least, it won't be her fault if you don't.

ROGERS. (*Politely*.) I don't quite follow you, I'm afraid.

ALAN. I'm sorry, sir. I was forgetting you're of an age to take care of yourself.

ROGERS. (*Testily*.) There's no need to call me 'sir', you know.

ALAN *raises his eyebrows*.

What you're implying is that this girl is – er – rather fast.

ALAN. I'm not implying it. I'm saying it. That girl is the fastest worker you're ever likely to see.

ROGERS. Oh! (*He goes back to his food*.)

BRIAN. (*Conciliatorily*.) What he means is that she's just naturally full of joie de vivre and all that. She's all right really. She just likes company.

ALAN. (*Under his breath*.) A battalion, you mean.

ROGERS. You sound embittered.

ALAN. Embittered? Oh, no. Oh, dear me, no. (*He breaks a roll open rather violently*.) Both Brian and I, for reasons that I won't go into now, are immune. Only I thought it just as well to let you know before you met her that Diana Lake, though a dear girl in many ways, is a little unreliable in her emotional life.

ROGERS. You mean she isn't in love with this chap Kit What's-his-name, who wants to marry her?

ALAN. The only reason I have for supposing she isn't is that she says that she is. But that's good enough for me.

Pause. BRIAN *gets up*.

BRIAN. Well, Maingot's simple French Phrases are calling me.

ROGERS. (*Evidently glad to change the subject*.) Maingot's Phrasebook. He's given me that to do, too.

BRIAN. Good. Then very soon now you will be able to walk into a chemist's and say in faultless French, 'Please, sir, I wish a toothpaste with a slightly stronger scent.'

ROGERS. Oh, really.

ALAN. Then think how nice it'll be if you're in a railway carriage, and you're able to inform a fellow traveller that the guard has just waved a red flag to signify that the locomotive has run off the line.

ROGERS. Sounds a bit out of date, I must say.

BRIAN. Maingot's grandfather wrote it, I believe.

The telephone rings. BRIAN *turns round.*

Do you know, I have a nasty feeling that's Chi-Chi.

ROGERS. Who's Chi-Chi?

BRIAN. That's not her real name.

MAINGOT*'s voice is heard from the garden.*

MAINGOT. (*Off.*) Monsieur Howard.

ALAN. (*Getting up, calling.*) Oui, Monsieur?

MAINGOT. (*Off.*) Voulez-vous répondre au téléphone, je vous en prie?

ALAN. Bien, Monsieur. (*He goes to telephone and takes off the receiver.*) Hullo . . . Bien. (*He holds out the receiver to* BRIAN.)

BRIAN. Me? Hell! (*He takes the receiver.*) Hullo . . . Ah hullo, Chi-Chi, comment ça va? Comment-allez-vous? . . . Quoi? . . . Quoi? . . . Wait a moment, Chi-Chi. (*Lowers receiver.*)

(*To* ALAN.) Take it for me, old boy. I can't hear a word the girl's saying.

ALAN *comes and takes it.*

ALAN. Hullo, Oui, il ne comprend pas . . . Bien. Je le lui demanderai.

(*To* BRIAN.) Can you see her tonight at the Casino? She wants you to meet her sister.

BRIAN. Ask her if it's the same one I met on Tuesday.

ALAN. (*In phone.*) Il voudrait savoir s'il a déjà rencontré votre soeur . . . Bon. (*To* BRIAN.) She says it's a different one.

BRIAN. Tell her it's O.K. I'll be there.

ALAN. (*In phone.*) Il dit qu'il sera enchanté . . . Oui . . . au revoir. (*He rings off.*)

BRIAN. I told that damn woman not to ring up here. (MAINGOT *enters from window.*)

MAINGOT. Alors. Qui est ce qui vient de téléphoner?

BRIAN. (*Apologetically.*) C'était quelqu'un pour moi, Monsieur.

MAINGOT. Pour vous?

BRIAN. Oui, une fille que je connais dans la ville.

MAINGOT. Une fille. (*He bursts into a stentorian roar of laughter and goes back into the garden.*) Une fille qu'il connait! Ho! Ho!

BRIAN. Now what's bitten him?

ALAN. A fille doesn't mean a girl, Brian.

BRIAN. It says so in my dictionary. What does it mean, then?

ALAN. A tart.

BRIAN. Oh! (*He considers a second.*) Well, I hate to have to say it, old boy, but having a strict regard for the truth that's a fairly neat little description of Chi-Chi. See you two at lunch time.

He goes out.

ALAN. There in a nutshell you have the reason for Brian's immunity to the charms of Diana Lake.

ROGERS. (*Icily.*) Really?

ALAN. (*Easily.*) Yes. (*Pause. He takes a cigarette.*) This place is going to be rather a change for you after your boat, isn't it?

ROGERS. (*Stung.*) You mean my ship, don't you?

ALAN. Oh, is there a difference?

ROGERS. There is.

ALAN. Of course. It's a grave social error to say boat for ship, isn't it? Like mentioning a lady's name before the royal toast or talking about Harrow College.

ROGERS. Yes, that would be very wrong.

DIANA LAKE *comes in from the garden. She is in a bathing wrap which she wears open, disclosing a bathing dress underneath. She is about twenty, very lovely.*

DIANA. Good morning. (*She stops at the sight of* ROGERS, *and decorously pulls her wrap more closely about her.*)

ROGERS *and* ALAN *get up.*

ALAN. Good morning, Diana. I don't think you've met Commander Rogers.

DIANA *comes forward and shakes hands.*

DIANA. How do you do?

ROGERS. How do you do?

DIANA. (*To* ROGERS.) I didn't know you'd – you must have arrived last night, I suppose?

ALAN. Don't you remember? You asked me what train he was coming by.

DIANA *comes round the table; kisses him on the top of his head.*

DIANA. Do sit down, Commander Rogers. (*He sits.*) How are you this morning, Alan?

ALAN. (*Feeling her bathing dress.*) I'll bet you didn't go in the water.

DIANA. Yes, I did.

ALAN. Right in?

DIANA. Yes, right in. Ask Kit.

ALAN. (*Really surprised.*) Kit? You don't mean to say that you got Kit to go bathing with you?

DIANA. Yes, I did. He's fetching my towel. I left it behind.

ALAN. God! you women.

DIANA. What?

ALAN. Without the slightest qualm and just to gratify a passing whim, you force a high-souled young man to shatter one of his most sacred principles.

ROGERS. What principle is that, if I might ask?

DIANA. (*Emphatically.*) Never, under any circumstances, to do anything hearty.

ROGERS. (*Challengingly.*) Personally, I rather like an early morning dip.

ALAN. (*As if the words burnt his mouth.*) An – early – morning – dip?

ROGERS. Certainly. That's hearty, I suppose.

ALAN. Well –

DIANA. I quite agree with you, Commander Rogers. I don't think there's anything nicer than a swim before breakfast. Ashtray? (*Hands it to* ROGERS.)

ALAN. You'd like anything that gave you a chance to come down to breakfast in a bathing dress.

DIANA. Does it shock you, Alan?

ALAN. Unutterably.

DIANA. I'll go and dress then.

ALAN. No. There's no point in that. You've made one successful entrance. Don't spoil it by making another.

ROGERS. I don't think I quite understand you.

ALAN. Diana does, don't you, angel?

DIANA. (*Sweetly.*) Has another publisher refused your novel, Alan?

ALAN, *momentarily disconcerted, can find nothing to say. Pause.*

Enter KIT *through the French window. He is about twenty-two, fair and good-looking. He wears a dressing-gown over his bathing dress, and carries two towels over his arm.*

KIT. (*Sullenly.*) Morning.

ALAN. (*In gentle reproof.*) Well, well, well.

KIT. (*Shamefacedly.*) Well, why not?

ALAN *shakes his head sadly.*

ALAN. I don't think you've met Commander Rogers.

KIT. (*Shaking hands.*) How do you do? I heard you were coming. (*He begins to dry his hair on a towel, throwing the other one to* DIANA.)

ALAN. Did Diana go in the water?

KIT. No.

DIANA. Kit, you dirty liar.

KIT. I've done enough for you already this morning I'm not going to perjure myself as well. (*He sits down gloomily and pours himself out a cup of coffee.*) I had hoped you wouldn't be here, Alan, to witness my shame.

ALAN. You of all people an early morning dipper.

KIT. (*Shuddering.*) Don't put it like that. You make it sound worse than it is. Say a nine o'clock bather. Oh, hell, this coffee's cold. Marianne!

ALAN. Mere toying with words can't hide the truth. Do you know I think that girl could make you go for a bicycle tour in the Pyrenees if she set her mind to it.

KIT. She could you know, Alan, that's the awful thing.

Slight pause.

ROGERS. I once went for a bicycle tour in the Pyrenees.

ALAN. Really?

KIT *splutters into his coffee simultaneously.*

JACQUELINE *comes out of the kitchen. She is about twenty-five or twenty-six, not unattractive, but nothing in looks to compare with* DIANA. *She wears an apron and has a handkerchief tied over her hair.*

JACQUELINE. Marianne's upstairs. Do you want anything? (*She speaks with only the barest trace of accent.*)

KIT. Hello, Jack.

ALAN. Good morning, darling.

JACQUELINE. (*Going to* ROGERS.) How do you do, Commander Rogers. I'm so glad you could come to us.

ROGERS. (*Shaking hands.*) Er – how do you do?

JACQUELINE. I hope you've found everything you want.

ROGERS. Yes, thank you.

JACQUELINE. Did Marianne ask you if you wanted eggs for breakfast?

ROGERS. I don't want any, thanks.

JACQUELINE. I see. Well, don't worry about asking for anything you need. By the way, do you drink beer at meals or do you prefer wine?

ROGERS. (*Sitting.*) Beer, please. Nothing like a can of beer.

ALAN. No, I suppose there isn't.

JACQUELINE. (*To* KIT.) What were you shouting about, by the way?

KIT. Jack, darling, the coffee's cold.

JACQUELINE. Of course it's cold. You're half an hour late for breakfast.

KIT. Yes, but . . .

JACQUELINE. You can't have any more because Marianne's doing the rooms.

KIT. I thought perhaps, Jack, darling, knowing how much you love me, you might be an angel and do something about it.

JACQUELINE. Certainly not. It's against all the rules of the house. Besides, you'd better go and get dressed. I'm giving you a lesson in five minutes.

KIT. In the near future, when I am Minister of Foreign Affairs, this incident will play a large part in my decision to declare war on France.

JACQUELINE *pushes him back into his chair and grabs the coffee-pot.*

JACQUELINE. Ooh! This is the last time I'm going to do this for you.

She goes back into the kitchen.

KIT. (*To* DIANA.) You see what a superb diplomat I should make.

ALAN. Rather the Palmerston tradition, wasn't it?

ROGERS. Was that Maingot's daughter?

KIT. Yes. Her name's Jacqueline.

ROGERS. Jacqueline? (*Brightly.*) I see. That's why you call her Jack.

KIT. (*Looking at him distastefully.*) Yes, that's why we call her Jack.

ROGERS. She speaks English very well.

KIT. She's been in England half her life. I believe she's going to be an English school-marm. You'll like her. She's amusing. (*He continues to dry himself.*) Hell! I still feel wet.

He glares at DIANA *who comes behind his chair and dries his hair with her own towel.*

DIANA. You've got such lovely hair, darling. That's why it takes so long to dry.

KIT. (*To* ALAN.) You know, Alan, this is a nice girl.

ALAN. (*Tilting his chair back and gazing at* DIANA.) Yes, she's nice. She's good, too.

ROGERS *gets up.*

ROGERS. Well, I must go upstairs. I want to get my room shipshape.

ALAN. And above board?

ROGERS. (*Turning savagely on* ALAN.) Yes, and above board. Any objection?

ALAN. (*Airily.*) No, no objection at all. Make it as above board as you like.

ROGERS. (*Bowing stiffly.*) Thank you. I'm most grateful.

Exit ROGERS.

ALAN. (*Pensively.*) Do you know, I don't think he likes me.

KIT. Who does? I'm the only one who can stand you and then only in small doses.

DIANA. Kenneth adores you, anyway. He's quite silly the way he tries to imitate you.

ALAN. Your brother shows remarkable acumen sometimes.

DIANA. And then, of course, I adore you too. You know that.

KIT *swings his chair round and pulls her roughly down on to his knee.*

KIT. Hey! I'm not going to have you adoring anybody except me. Do you understand? (*He kisses her.*)

DIANA. Darling, you're not jealous of Alan, are you?

KIT. I'm jealous of anyone you even look at.

DIANA. All right, then in future I won't look at anyone except you.

KIT. That's a promise?

DIANA. That's a promise.

ALAN, *still leaning back in his chair, whistles a tune softly.*

(*Feeling* KIT*'s hands.*) Darling, you *are* cold.

KIT. Yes, I know. I think I'll go and dress and not wait for the coffee. (*He gets up.*) You've probably given me pneumonia. But I don't mind. You could tear me up in little pieces and trample on them, and I'd still love you.

DIANA. Sweet little thing. Take these things upstairs, darling, will you? (*Gives him towels.*)

KIT *goes out.*

ALAN. That's no reason why you should, you know.

DIANA. Should what?

ALAN. Tear him up in little pieces and trample on them.

DIANA *crosses over to the window where she stands, looking out.*

So you're not going to look at anyone except Kit.

DIANA *doesn't answer.* ALAN *gets up and walks over to the window. He puts his arm round her waist and his cheek against her.*

(*After a pause.*) This doesn't mean I'm falling for you.

DIANA. (*Gently.*) Doesn't it, Alan?

ALAN. No, it doesn't.

He walks over to the armchair and sits.

DIANA. I am disappointed.

ALAN. What do you think of the Commander?

DIANA. I think he's quite nice.

ALAN. Yes. (*Gently.*) Yes. I want to tell you, it's no good starting anything with him.

DIANA. Don't be silly, Alan.

ALAN. It really isn't any good, darling, because you see I've warned him against you.

DIANA. You warned him? (*Coming to* ALAN.) What did you say?

ALAN. I told him what you are.

DIANA. (*Quietly.*) What's that?

ALAN. Don't you know?

DIANA. Alan, much as I like you there *are* times when I could cheerfully strangle you.

ALAN. Is this one of them, darling?

DIANA. Yes, ducky, it is.

ALAN. Good, that's just what I hoped.

DIANA. This is rather a new rôle for you, isn't it, playing wet nurse to the Navy?

ALAN. You don't think it suits me?

DIANA. No, darling, I'm afraid I don't. What are you doing it for?

ALAN. It's not because I'm fond of the Commander. As a matter of fact it would rather amuse me to see you play hell with the Commander. But I do like Kit, that's why. So no hanky-panky with the Navy or . . .

DIANA. Or what?

ALAN. Or I shall have to be rather beastly to you, darling, and you know you wouldn't like that.

DIANA. You don't understand me at all, Alan.

ALAN. I understand every little bit of you, Diana, through and through. That's why we get along so well together.

DIANA. (*Tearfully.*) I ought to *hate* you.

ALAN. Well, go on trying, darling, and you may succeed. (*He kisses her on the back of the neck.*) I've got to go and finish some stuff for Maingot. See you at lunch time. (*He goes to the door.*)

DIANA. Alan?

ALAN. (*Turning at door.*) Yes?

DIANA. What do you mean by hanky-panky?

ALAN. *I* should tell *you.*

He goes out.

DIANA *kicks petulantly at the window. She goes to the table, opens her handbag, takes out a small mirror and looks at herself.*

Enter JACQUELINE *from the kitchen with the coffee-pot.*

DIANA. Oh, thank you so much.

JACQUELINE. Where's Kit?

DIANA. He's gone up to dress. He felt cold.

JACQUELINE. Isn't that like him. Well, you can tell him that I'm not going to make him any more coffee however loud he screams.

DIANA. Yes, I'll tell him, and I think you're quite right.

Enter ROGERS *through the door at the back.*

ROGERS. (*Nervously.*) Oh, hullo.

JACQUELINE *goes out into the kitchen.*

DIANA. (*Brightly.*) Hullo, Commander Rogers.

ROGERS *goes over to the bookcase at the back.*

Looking for something?

ROGERS. Yes, Maingot's Phrase Book, as a matter of fact. (*He bends down and pulls a book out.*) Here it is, I think. (*He looks at the title.*) No, it isn't.

DIANA. Let me help you. I think I know where it is.

ROGERS. Oh, that's very good of you.

DIANA *bends down at the bookcase and pulls a book out.*

DIANA. Here. (*She hands it to him.*)

ROGERS. Oh, thanks most awfully.

DIANA. (*Going back to the table.*) Well, what are your first impressions of Monsieur Maingot's establishment?

ROGERS. Oh, I – er – think it ought to be very cheery here.

DIANA. I'm sure you'll love it.

ROGERS. Yes, I'm sure I will.

DIANA. The boys are so nice, don't you think?

ROGERS. Er – yes, I think they are – some of them. (*He makes a tentative move towards the door.*)

DIANA. (*Quickly.*) I suppose you find Alan a bit startling, don't you?

ROGERS. Alan?

DIANA. The one with the German coat.

ROGERS. Oh, yes. Yes, he is a bit startling. Well, I ought to be getting along.

DIANA. Why? You've got your room pretty well shipshape by now, haven't you?

ROGERS. Oh, thanks, yes, I have.

DIANA. Well, don't go for a bit. Stay and talk to me while I have my coffee. Have you got a cigarette?

ROGERS. (*Coming to her.*) Yes, I have. (*Offers her one.*)

DIANA. (*Takes one.*) Thanks. I was saying about Alan –

ROGERS. Match?

DIANA. Thanks. (*He lights it.*) What was I saying?

ROGERS. About Alan.

DIANA. Oh, yes, about Alan – he's really very nice but you mustn't take everything he says seriously.

ROGERS. Oh. Oh, I see. No, I won't.

DIANA. He's just the tiniest bit – you know (*She taps her forehead significantly.*) unbalanced.

ROGERS. Oh, really.

DIANA. I thought it as well to warn you.

ROGERS. Yes. Thank you very much.

DIANA. Otherwise it might lead to trouble.

ROGERS. Yes, it might.

Pause.

DIANA. Poor Alan. I'm afraid he's got it very badly.

ROGERS. Er – got what?

DIANA. Well – (*She leans back and blows a puff of smoke into the air.*) Of course I oughtn't to say it. (*Pause. She throws him a quick glance to see if he has caught her meaning. Evidently he hasn't.*)

ROGERS. Oh.

DIANA. I'm awfully sorry for him of course.

ROGERS. (*Puzzled, but polite.*) Of course.

DIANA. It's so funny, because from the way he behaves to me and the things he says about me, you'd think he hated me, wouldn't you?

ROGERS. Yes, you would. (*Pause.*) Doesn't he?

DIANA. (*Laughing.*) No. Oh no. Far from it.

ROGERS. (*The light of understanding in his face at last.*) Oh, I see. You mean he's rather keen on you?

DIANA. I mustn't give him away. It wouldn't be fair. But if he ever talks to you about me, as he probably will, and tries to give you the impression that I'm a (*smiling*) scheming wrecker of men's lives, you needn't necessarily believe him.

ROGERS. No – no, I won't, of course. But I don't see why he should, you know.

DIANA. (*Embarrassedly.*) Well, you see, Commander Rogers, I like Alan, but I don't like him as much as perhaps he wants me to, and I suppose that makes him feel rather embittered.

ROGERS. Ah, yes. I see.

DIANA. (*Gaily.*) Well, don't let's talk any more about it, because it's not a very pleasant subject. Tell me about yourself. Tell me about the Navy. I'm always thrilled to death by anything to do with the sea.

ROGERS. Really, that's splendid.

Pause.

DIANA. It must be a wonderful life.

ROGERS. Yes, it's a pretty good life on the whole.

DIANA. Marvellously interesting, I should think.

ROGERS. Yes, pretty interesting.

DIANA. I bet you've had any amount of wildly exciting experiences.

ROGERS. Oh, well, you know, things have a way of happening in the Navy.

DIANA. Yes, I'm sure they have. (*Pause.*) You naval people never talk about yourselves, do you?

ROGERS. Well, you know, silent service and all that.

DIANA. Yes, I know, but I do hope you're not going to be too silent with me, because honestly, I am so terribly interested.

ROGERS. (*Smiling.*) I'll try not to be too silent then.

Pause.

DIANA. What are you doing this morning?

ROGERS. Nothing special. Why?

DIANA. How would you like to have a look round the town?

Enter JACQUELINE *from the kitchen.*

JACQUELINE. Hasn't Kit come down yet?

ROGERS. (*To* DIANA.) Oh, I'd love to.

DIANA. Good. I'll go and get dressed and we'll go for a little stroll.

ROGERS. But isn't it rather a bore for you?

DIANA. No, of course not. I'd love it. (*She goes to the door.*)

JACQUELINE. Diana?

DIANA. Yes?

JACQUELINE. (*Pouring out a cup of coffee.*) If you're going past Kit's room you might give him this. (*She hands her the cup.*)

DIANA. Right, I will. (*To* ROGERS.) Are you sure I'm not dragging you away from your work or anything?

JACQUELINE *goes back into the kitchen.*

ROGERS. Oh, no. That's quite all right. I haven't been given anything to do yet.

DIANA. Good. Well, I'll go and put some clothes on.

She turns to go. ALAN *comes in and almost collides with her in the doorway.*

(*Turning.*) I'll meet you down here then in about a quarter of an hour?

ROGERS. Right.

DIANA *smiles at* ROGERS, *walks past* ALAN *without glancing at him and goes out.*

ALAN. (*Going to the table and sitting.*) Going for a little constitutional, Commander? (*He has some books in his hands. He places them on the table in front of him and opens a notebook.*)

ROGERS. Yes. (*He turns his back.*)

ALAN. (*Taking a fountain pen from his pocket and unscrewing the top.*) You've got a nice day for it. (*Pause. He writes in his notebook and begins to sing the Lorelei. Without looking up.*) It's a lovely song, the Lorelei, don't you think?

ROGERS. It *could* be.

ALAN. True. (*He continues to write.*) It's a stupid fable anyway. I ask you, what sailor would be lured to his doom after he had been warned of his danger?

ROGERS. (*Turning quickly.*) If you think that's funny, I don't.

Enter KENNETH *through the window.*

KENNETH. Oh, Commander Rogers, Maingot wants to see you a moment.

Pause. ROGERS *is standing facing* ALAN *across the table, and* ALAN *is still writing.*

ROGERS. Right. Thank you. (*He marches out into the garden.*)

ALAN. (*After a pause.*) Well, Babe, I suppose you were murdered by the old man.

KENNETH. (*Wearily.*) More so than usual this morning.

Pause. ALAN *goes on writing.*

ALAN. (*Without looking up.*) Babe, I don't like your sister.

KENNETH. (*Walking round the table and looking over* ALAN*'s shoulder at what he is writing.*) Don't you? I thought you did like her, rather a lot.

ALAN *looks up. Pause.*

Enter JACQUELINE *from the kitchen. She has taken off her apron and the handkerchief over her hair.*

JACQUELINE. Good morning, Kenneth.

KENNETH. Good morning, Mam'selle.

JACQUELINE. Had your lesson?

KENNETH. Yes. I've got to do the whole damn thing again. (*He goes to the door.*) Alan, I wish to God I had your brains.

He goes out. ALAN *looks after him a moment, then goes back to his work.*

JACQUELINE. (*Looking at her watch.*) Kit is a monster. He's never been on time for his lesson yet. (*She goes to the window and looks out.*)

ALAN. (*Looking up from his work.*) What have you done to your hair: Jack?

JACQUELINE. (*Turning round.*) Do you like it? (*Her hair is done in the same way as* DIANA*'s.*)

ALAN. (*He gets up and walks over to her, holding her out at arm's length and studying her hair. Doubtfully.*) No, it's a mistake, Jack. You won't beat her by copying the way she does her hair.

JACQUELINE. He'll like it, Alan, I'm sure he will.

ALAN. He won't notice it.

JACQUELINE. He will, you see.

ALAN. I'll bet you five francs he doesn't.

JACQUELINE. All right. That's a bet.

ALAN. Go and change it while there's still time. Make it look hideous like it used to.

JACQUELINE. (*Laughing*.) No, Alan.

Pause.

ALAN. Poor Jack. I must find you someone else to fall in love with.

JACQUELINE. So long as you don't tell him that I adore him, I don't mind what you do.

ALAN. Anyone less half-witted than Kit would have seen it years ago.

JACQUELINE. Am I very obvious, Alan? I don't want to bore him.

ALAN. Go and change that hair.

JACQUELINE. Do you think if Diana were out of the way I should stand a chance?

ALAN. You're not thinking of putting her out of the way, are you?

JACQUELINE. (*Smiling*.) I'd do it painlessly, Alan.

ALAN. Why painlessly?

JACQUELINE. I'm not jealous of her really, though.

ALAN. Oh, no. Not a bit.

JACQUELINE. Honestly, Alan, I wouldn't mind if she made him happy. But she doesn't. She seems to enjoy making him miserable. And now that the Commander's here it's going to be much worse. You know what I mean, don't you?

ALAN. I have an idea.

JACQUELINE. Can't we do anything about it, Alan?

ALAN. Yes. Go and change that hair, Jack. It's the only chance.

JACQUELINE. No, I won't do anything of the sort.

Enter KIT, *dressed*.

KIT. (*Walking right up to* JACQUELINE *and taking her hands earnestly*.) Jack, I have something to tell you. (*To* ALAN.) Go away, Alan, this is confidential.

ALAN *goes back to the table and his work.*

JACQUELINE. What is it, Kit?

KIT. I haven't done that work you set me.

JACQUELINE. Oh, Kit. Why not?

KIT. Well, I took Diana to the Casino last night, and –

JACQUELINE. Kit, really –

KIT. But as a great treat I'll translate you some La Bruyère this morning. Come on. (*He pulls her towards one of the armchairs.*)

JACQUELINE. I set you that work specially because I thought it would interest you, and anyway you can't afford to slack off just now before your exam.

KIT. (*Hands a her book.*) Now sit down and read your nice La Bruyère and be quiet. Are you comfortable? (*Opening his own book.*) Page one hundred and eight. Listen, Alan. You can learn a lot from hearing French beautifully translated. Chapter four. (*Translating.*) Of the heart . . .

JACQUELINE. Of love.

KIT. Of love, then. (*Translating.*) There is a fragrance in pure love . . .

JACQUELINE. In pure friendship.

KIT. (*Translating.*) Friendship can exist between people of different sexes.

ALAN. You don't say.

KIT. I don't. La Bruyère does. (*Translating.*) Friendship can exist between people of different sexes, quite exempt from all grossness.

JACQUELINE. Quite free from all . . .

ALAN. Hanky-panky.

JACQUELINE. Quite free from all unworthy thoughts.

KIT. Quite exempt from all grossness. (*Looking up.*) I know what it is. It's been bothering me all the time. You've changed your hair, haven't you, Jack?

JACQUELINE. (*Giving ALAN a quick glance.*) Yes, Kit, I've changed my hair.

KIT. Alan, do look at Jack. She's changed her hair.

ALAN. (*Looking up.*) So she has. Well – well – well.

KIT. I knew you'd done something to yourself. (*He studies her.*) It's queer, you know. It makes you look quite . . .

JACQUELINE. (*Eagerly.*) Quite what, Kit?

KIT. I was going to say alluring.

He laughs as if he'd made a joke; JACQUELINE *laughs, too.*

JACQUELINE. You do like it, anyway, Kit?

KIT. Yes, I do. I think it's very nice.

JACQUELINE. You think I ought to keep it like this?

Before KIT *can answer,* ROGERS *has appeared from garden.*

ROGERS. Sorry, Maingot wants to take me now, so would one of you mind telling Diana – er – I mean Miss Lake, that we'll have to postpone our walk?

Pause.

ALAN. Yes, I'll tell her.

ROGERS. Thank you.

He goes back into garden.

JACQUELINE. (*Breaking a silence.*) You think I ought to keep it like this?

KIT. (*Turning slowly.*) Keep what?

JACQUELINE. My hair.

KIT. Oh, don't be such a bore about your hair, Jack. Yes, keep it like that. It'll get a laugh anyway.

He goes out quickly. Pause. JACQUELINE *closes her book with a slam and rises.*

JACQUELINE. Five francs please, Alan.

Curtain.

Act Two, Scene One

Scene: same as Act One.

Time: a fortnight later, about 2 p.m.

Lunch is just finished. All the characters seen in Act One are still sitting at the table. MAINGOT *sits at one end,* ALAN *facing him at the other end. On* MAINGOT's *right are* ROGERS, DIANA, *and* KIT, *in that order, facing the audience. On his left are* BRIAN, KENNETH, *and* JACQUELINE, *also in that order, with their backs to the audience. On the rise of the curtain conversation is general.* ALAN *is talking to* JACQUELINE, BRIAN *to* MAINGOT, *and* ROGERS *to* DIANA. *After a few seconds conversation lapses and* ROGERS' *voice can be heard.*

ROGERS. Oh, yes, Tuppy Jones. Yes, he's in Belligerent. I know him quite well. Cheery cove. (*He chuckles.*) There's an amusing story about him as a matter of fact. He got a bit tight in Portsmouth, and broke seven Belisha Beacons with an air pistol.

MAINGOT. (*Turning politely to* ROGERS.) Eh, bien, Monsieur le Commandant, voulez-vous raconter votre petite histoire en français? Please to tell your little story in French.

ROGERS. (*Confused.*) Oh, no, sir. That's a bit unfair. I don't know enough.

MAINGOT. You should have learnt enough, my Commander.

ROGERS. But, dash it, sir, I've only been here a few days.

MAINGOT. Two weeks, my Commander. After two weeks my pupils are usually enough advanced to tell me little stories in French.

ROGERS. Well, I'm afraid I can't tell this one, sir. It wasn't a story anyway.

ALAN. (*Leaning forward malevolently.*) Au contraire, Monsieur, l'histoire de Monsieur le Commandant était excessivement rigolo.

MAINGOT. Bien. Alors, racontez-la vous même.

ALAN. Il parâit qu'il connait un type qui s'appelle Tuppy Jones. Alors ce bonhomme, se promenant un soir par les rues de Portsmouth, et ayant un peu trop bu, a brisé, à coups de pistolet à vent, sept Belisha Beacons.

MAINGOT. (*Who has been listening attentively, his ear cupped in his hand.*) Et puis?

ALAN. C'est tout, Monsieur.

MAINGOT. C'est tout?

KIT. Vous savez que ce Tuppy Jones était d'un esprit le plus fin du monde.

MAINGOT. Je crois bien. Au même temps, je n'ai pas tout à fait compris. Qu'est-ce que ça veut dire – Belisha Beacons?

ALAN. Ah, ça c'est un peu compliqué.

BRIAN. (*Showing off his French.*) Belisha Beacons sont des objets – (*He stops.*)

ALAN. Qui se trouvent actuellement dans les rues de Londres –

KIT. Et qui sont dédiés au salut des passants.

MAINGOT. Aha. Des emblemes religieux?

ALAN. C'est ça. Des emblèmes religieux.

MAINGOT. (*To* ROGERS.) So one finds it funny in England to break these religious emblems with a wind pistol?

ROGERS. (*Not having understood.*) Well – (MAINGOT *shrugs his shoulders sadly.*)

(*Angrily* to ALAN.) Damn you, Howard.

BRIAN. That's not fair.

ALAN. It was a very good story, I thought.

MAINGOT. (*Rising, having finished his wine.*) Bien, Messieurs, Mesdames, la session est terminée. (*He gets up.* ALL *get up after him.*)

(*Holding up his hand.*) One moment please. I speak in English for those who cannot understand. How many of you are going tonight to the Costume Ball and great battle of flowers at the Casino? Please hold up your hands.

KIT. (*To* ALAN.) Good lord! Is it July the fourteenth? I'd no idea.

All hold up their hands.

MAINGOT. All of you! Good. The festivities commence at eight o'clock; there will be no dinner 'ere. All right.

MAINGOT *moves to window and stops.*

One moment, please. I give my history lecture at two-thirty, that is to say in twenty minutes' time. All right.

He goes out into garden.

ROGERS *and* DIANA *are moving towards the French windows.* KIT *catches them up.*

KIT. (*To* DIANA.) What about a game of Japanese billiards, Diana?

DIANA. (*Indicating* ROGERS.) Bill's just asked me to play, Kit. I'll play you afterwards. Come on, Bill.

ROGERS. Sorry, Neilan.

ROGERS *and* DIANA *go out together.* KIT *goes to an armchair and sits sulkily.* BRIAN *has pulled out a wallet and is fumbling inside it.* ALAN *is going out through the window when* KENNETH *catches him up.*

KENNETH. Alan, will you help me with that essay now? You said you would.

ALAN. Oh hell! Can't you do it yourself?

KENNETH. Well, I could, but it might mean missing this dance tonight, and I'd hate that. Do help me. It's on Robespierre, and I know nothing about him.

ALAN. There's a chapter on him in Lavisse. Why don't you copy that out? The old man won't notice. He'll probably say that it isn't French, but still –

He goes out.

KENNETH. (*Shouting after him.*) Alan, be a sportsman.

ALAN. (*Off.*) Nothing I should hate more.

KENNETH. Oh, hell!

KENNETH *turns sadly and goes past* KIT *to the door at the back.*

KIT. (*Moodily.*) What Alan wants is a good kick in the pants.

KENNETH. (*At door.*) Oh, I don't know.

He goes out. BRIAN *puts his wallet back in his pocket.*

BRIAN. I say, old boy, I suppose you couldn't lend me fifty francs, could you?

KIT. No, I couldn't. At any rate, not until you've paid me back that hundred you owe me.

BRIAN. Ah, I see your point. (*Cheerfully.*) Well, old boy, no ill feelings. I'll have to put off Chi-Chi for tonight, that's all.

KIT. You weren't thinking of taking her to this thing at the Casino, were you?

BRIAN. Yes.

KIT. What do you think Maingot would have said if he'd seen her?

BRIAN. That would have been all right. I told him I was taking the daughter of the British Consul.

KIT. But she doesn't exactly look like the daughter of the British Consul, does she?

BRIAN. Well, after all, it's fancy dress. It's just possible the daughter of the British Consul might go dressed as Nana of the Boulevards. Still, I admit that if he'd actually met her he might have found it odd that the only English she knew was ' I love you, Big Boy'.

KIT. How do you manage to talk to her, then?

BRIAN. Oh, we get along, old boy, we get along. (*Going to window.*) You couldn't make it thirty francs, I suppose?

KIT. No, and I don't suppose Chi-Chi could either.

BRIAN. Oh, well, you may be right. I'd better pop round in the car and tell her I won't be there tonight.

KIT. Oh, listen, Brian, if you want someone to take, why don't you take Jack?

BRIAN. Isn't anyone taking her?

KIT. Yes, I'm supposed to be, but –

BRIAN. (*Surprised.*) You, old boy? What about Diana?

KIT. Oh, she's being taken by the Commander.

BRIAN. Oh.

Pause.

As a matter of fact, I don't think I'll go at all. I don't fancy myself at a battle of flowers.

KIT. Nor do I, if it comes to that.

BRIAN. Oh, I don't know. I think you'd hurl a prettier bloom than I would. Well, so long.

He goes out. KIT *sits biting his nails. The ferocious din of a sports car tuning up comes through the window.* KIT *jumps up.*

KIT. (*Shouting through the window.*) Must you make all that noise?

BRIAN. (*Off, his voice coming faintly above the din.*) Can't hear, old boy.

The noise lessens as the car moves off down the street. JACQUELINE *and* MARIANNE *come in, the latter bearing a tray.*

KIT. (*Turning.*) God knows why Brian finds it necessary to have a car that sounds like – like five dictators all talking at once.

JACQUELINE. (*Helping* MARIANNE *clear.*) It goes with his character, Kit. He'd think it was effeminate to have a car that was possible to sit in without getting cramp and that didn't deafen one.

KIT. (*Sitting again.*) I wonder what it's like to be as hearty as Brian?

JACQUELINE. Awful, I should think.

KIT. No, I should think very pleasant. Have you ever seen Brian bad-tempered?

JACQUELINE. No, but then I think he's too stupid to be bad-tempered.

KIT. It doesn't follow. Cats and dogs are bad-tempered, sometimes. No, Brian may be stupid but he's right-minded. He's solved the problem of living better than any of us.

MARIANNE *goes out with a loaded tray.*

It seems a simple solution, too. All it needs, apparently, is the occasional outlay of fifty francs. I wish I could do the same.

JACQUELINE. I expect you could if you tried.

KIT. I have tried. Often.

JACQUELINE *is folding up the table-cloth.*

Does that shock you?

JACQUELINE. Why should it?

KIT. I just wondered.

JACQUELINE. I'm a woman of the world.

KIT. (*Smiling.*) That's the last thing you are. But I'll tell you this, Jack. I like you so much that it's sometimes quite an effort to remember that you're a woman at all.

JACQUELINE. Oh.

She puts the table-cloth in a drawer of the table and shuts it with something of a slam.

I thought you liked women.

KIT. I don't think one likes women, does one? One loves them sometimes, but that's a different thing altogether. Still, I like you. That's what's so odd.

JACQUELINE. (*Brightly.*) Thank you, Kit. I like you, too.

KIT. Good. That's nice for both of us, isn't it?

He returns his gaze to the window. JACQUELINE, *in a sudden fit of temper, kicks the leg of the table.*

Clumsy!

JACQUELINE. (*Limping over to the other armchair and sitting.*) Have you found anything to wear tonight?

KIT. Supposing I didn't go, would you mind?

JACQUELINE. Well, I have been rather looking forward to tonight.

KIT. Alan could take you. He's a better dancer than I am.

JACQUELINE. (*After a pause.*) Why don't you wear that Greek dress of my brother's?

KIT. Jack, you know, I don't think I could cope with a battle of flowers. (*He turns and meets her eyes.*) Could I get into this dress of your brother's?

JACQUELINE. Yes, easily. It may be a bit tight.

ALAN *comes in through the window.*

KIT. That reminds me. I hope there'll be plenty to drink at this affair.

ALAN. (*Morosely.*) There's nothing else for it. I shall have to murder that man.

JACQUELINE. Who?

ALAN. The Commander.

KIT. Surely that's my privilege, isn't it?

ALAN. I've just been watching him play Japanese billiards with Diana. Now you would think, wouldn't you, that Japanese billiards was a fairly simple game? You either roll wooden balls into holes or you don't. That should be the end of it. But as played by the Commander it becomes a sort of naval battle. Every shot he makes is either a plunging salvo or a blasting broadside, or a direct hit amidships.

KIT. At least he has the excuse that it amuses Diana. (*He gets up.*) Will you explain to me, Alan, as an impartial observer, how she can bear to be more than two minutes in that man's company?

ALAN. Certainly. He's in the process of falling in love with her.

KIT. Yes, that's obvious, but –

ALAN. When one hooks a salmon one has to spend a certain amount of time playing it. If one doesn't, it escapes.

KIT. Is that meant to be funny?

ALAN. Of course. When the salmon is landed, all that's necessary is an occasional kick to prevent it slipping back into the water.

KIT. (*Angrily.*) Don't be a damned fool.

ALAN. Tomorrow a certain Lord Heybrook is arriving. Diana is naturally rather anxious to bring the Commander to the gaff as quickly as possible, so that she can have two nice fat fish gasping and squirming about on the bank, before she starts to fish for what'll be the best catch of all of you, if she can bring it off.

Pause. KIT *suddenly bursts out laughing.*

KIT. No wonder you can't get anyone to take your novel.

ALAN. (*Hurt.*) I can't quite see what my novel has got to do with the machinations of a scalp-hunter.

JACQUELINE *rises in alarm.*

KIT. (*Walking over to* ALAN.) Listen, Alan. One more crack like that –

JACQUELINE. (*Hurriedly, to* ALAN.) Kit's quite right. You shouldn't say things like that.

KIT. (*Turning to her savagely.*) What do you know about it, anyway?

JACQUELINE. Nothing, only –

KIT. Well, please go away. This is between Alan and me.

JACQUELINE. Oh, I'm sorry.

JACQUELINE *goes into garden.*

KIT. Now. Will you please understand this. I am in love with Diana, and Diana is in love with me. Now that's not too hard for you to grasp, is it? Because I'll repeat it again slowly if you like.

ALAN. (*Genially.*) No, no. I've read about that sort of thing in books. The Commander, of course, is just an old friend who's known her since she was so high.

KIT. The Commander's in love with her, but you can't blame Diana for that.

ALAN. Of course I don't. It was a very smart piece of work on her part.

KIT. (*Swallowing his anger.*) She's too kind-hearted to tell him to go to hell –

ALAN. I suppose it's because she's so kind-hearted that she calls him 'darling', and plays these peculiar games with him all over the place.

Pause.

KIT. I called you an impartial observer a moment ago. Well, you're not. I believe you're in love with Diana yourself.

ALAN. My dear Kit! As a matter of fact, I admit it's quite possible I shall end by marrying her.

KIT. You'll what?

ALAN. But that'll only be – to take another sporting metaphor – like the stag who turns at bay through sheer exhaustion at being hunted.

Pause.

KIT. (*Aggressively.*) God! Alan, I've a good mind to –

ALAN. I shouldn't. It'd make us both look rather silly.

DIANA *and* ROGERS *heard off in garden.*

Besides, you know how strongly I disapprove of fighting over a woman.

DIANA *appears at window,* ROGERS *following.*

ROGERS. (*Coming in through window.*) Well, of course, there was only one thing to do. So I gave the order – all hands on deck – (*Stops at sight of* KIT *and* ALAN.)

ALAN. And did they come?

ROGERS. (*Ignoring* ALAN, *to* DIANA.) Let's go out in the garden, Diana.

DIANA. (*Languidly throwing herself into an armchair.*) It's so hot, Bill. Let's stay here.

KIT. Aren't you going to play me a game of Japanese billiards, Diana?

DIANA. You don't mind, do you, Kit? I'm quite exhausted as a matter of fact.

KIT. (*Furious.*) Oh, no. I don't mind a bit.

He goes out into the garden. Pause. ALAN *begins to hum the Lorelei.* ROGERS *walks towards window.*

ALAN. Don't leave us, Commander. If one of us has to go, let it be myself.

ROGERS *stops.* ALAN *walks to door at back.*

I shall go aloft.

He goes out.

ROGERS. Silly young fool. I'd like to have him in my ship. Do him all the good in the world.

DIANA. Yes. It might knock some of the conceit out of him.

ROGERS. Y-e-s. Has he been – bothering you at all lately?

DIANA. (*With a gesture of resignation.*) Oh, well. I'm awfully sorry for him, you know.

ROGERS. I find it hard to understand you sometimes, Diana.

He sits in chair beside her. She pats his hand.

At least I think I do understand you, but if you don't mind me saying it, I think you're too kind-hearted – far too kind-hearted.

DIANA. (*With a sigh.*) Yes, I think I am.

ROGERS. For instance – I can't understand why you don't tell Kit.

DIANA. (*Rising.*) Oh, Bill, please –

ROGERS. I'm sorry to keep on at you about it, Diana, but you don't know how much I resent him behaving as if you were still in love with him.

DIANA. But I can't tell him – not yet, anyway. (*Gently.*) Surely you must see how cruel that would be?

ROGERS. This is a case where you must be cruel only to be kind.

DIANA. Yes, Bill, that's true. Terribly true. But you know, cruelty is something that's physically impossible to me. I'm the sort of person who's miserable if I tread on a snail.

ROGERS. You must tell him, Diana. Otherwise it's so unfair on him. Tell him now.

DIANA. (*Quickly.*) No, not now.

ROGERS. Well, this evening.

DIANA. Well, I'll try. It's a terribly hard thing to do. It's like – it's like kicking someone when he's down.

ROGERS *puts his arms round her.*

ROGERS. I know, old girl, it's a rotten thing to have to do. Poor little thing, you mustn't think I don't sympathise with you, you know.

DIANA. (*Laying her head on his chest.*) Oh, Bill, I do feel such a beast.

ROGERS. Yes, yes, of course. But these things happen, you know.

DIANA. I can't understand it even yet. I loved Kit – at least I thought I did, and then you happened – and – and – Oh, Bill, do you do this to all the women you meet?

ROGERS. Er – do what?

DIANA. Sweep them off their feet so that they forget everything in the world except yourself.

ROGERS. Diana, will you give me a truthful answer to a question I'm going to ask you?

DIANA. Yes, of course, Bill.

ROGERS. Is your feeling for me mere – infatuation, or do you really, really love me?

DIANA. Oh, you know I do, Bill.

ROGERS. (*He kisses her.*) Oh, darling. And you really don't love Kit any more?

DIANA. I'm still fond of him.

ROGERS. But you don't love him?

DIANA. No, Bill, I don't love him.

JACQUELINE *comes in through the window.* ROGERS, *his back to her, doesn't see her.* DIANA *breaks away.*

ROGERS. And you *will* tell him so?

DIANA. Hullo, Jacqueline.

JACQUELINE. Hullo, Diana. Rather warm, isn't it?

She walks across the room and into the kitchen.

DIANA. (*Alarmed.*) You don't think she saw anything, do you?

ROGERS. I don't know.

DIANA. She may have been standing outside the window the whole time. I wouldn't put it past her.

ROGERS. What does it matter anyway? Everyone will know soon enough.

DIANA. (*Thoughtfully.*) She's the sort of girl who'll talk.

ROGERS. Let her.

DIANA. (*Turning to him.*) Bill, you don't understand. Our feelings for each other are too sacred to be soiled by vulgar gossip.

ROGERS. Er – yes, yes. But, dash it, we can't go on keeping it a secret for ever.

DIANA. Not for ever. But don't you find it thrilling to have such a lovely secret just between us and no one else? After all, it's our love. Why should others know about it and bandy it about?

ROGERS. Yes, I know, but –

KIT *comes in through window. He glances moodily at* DIANA *and* ROGERS *and throws himself into an armchair, picking up a paper and beginning to read.* ROGERS *points significantly at him and frames the words 'Tell him now' in his mouth.* DIANA *shakes her head violently.* ROGERS *nods his head urgently.* KIT *looks up.*

DIANA. (*Hurriedly.*) You people have got a lecture now, haven't you?

KIT. In about five minutes.

DIANA. Oh. Then I think I'll go for a little walk by myself. (*Going to window.*) We'll have our bathe about four, don't you think, Bill?

ROGERS. Right.

DIANA *goes out. Pause.*

(*Breezily.*) Well, Neilan, how's the world treating you these days.

KIT. Bloodily.

ROGERS. I'm sorry to hear that. What's the trouble?

KIT. Everything. (*He takes up a paper.*)

ROGERS. (*After a pause.*) This show tonight at the Casino ought to be rather cheery, don't you think?

KIT *lowers his paper, looks at him, and raises it again.*

Who are you taking?

KIT. (*Into the paper.*) Jacqueline.

ROGERS. Jacqueline?

KIT. (*Loudly.*) Yes, Jacqueline.

ROGERS. Oh. (*Cheerfully.*) That's a charming girl, I think. Clever. Amusing. Pretty. She'll make somebody a fine wife.

KIT *emits a kind of snort.*

Did you say anything?

KIT *doesn't answer.*

She's what the French call a sympathetic person.

KIT. Do they? I didn't know.

ROGERS. Oh, yes they do. Much nicer than most modern girls. Take some of these English girls, for instance –

KIT. You take them. I want to read.

He turns his back. ROGERS, *annoyed, shrugs his shoulders.* BRIAN's *car is heard outside in the road.* ROGERS *goes to the bookcase and takes out his notebook.*

BRIAN*'s voice can be heard in the garden singing 'Somebody Stole my Girl'.*

KIT *gets up.*

(*Shouting through the window.*) Blast you, Brian.

BRIAN. (*Appearing at window.*) What's the matter, old boy? Don't you like my voice?

KIT. No, and I don't like that song.

BRIAN. 'Somebody Stole my Girl'? Why, it's a – (*He looks from* KIT *to* ROGERS.) Perhaps you're right. It's not one of my better efforts. (*He puts a parcel on the table.*) This has just come for Alan. It feels suspiciously like his novel. (*He goes to bookcase and takes out his notebook.*) You won't believe it, but I used to sing in my school choir. Only because I was in the rugger fifteen, I admit. (*Sits next* KIT.) What's the old boy lecturing on today?

KIT. The Near East, I suppose. He didn't finish it yesterday.

BRIAN. Good lord! Was it the Near East yesterday? I thought it was the Franco-Prussian War.

KIT. You must get a lot of value out of these lectures.

BRIAN. Well, I only understood one word in a hundred.

ROGERS. It's rather the same in my case.

BRIAN. Give me your notes in case the old boy has the impertinence to ask me a question.

He takes KIT*'s notes and starts to read them.* ALAN *comes in through door at the back, followed by* KENNETH.

ALAN. (*Going to table and picking up parcel.*) Ah, I see the novel has come home to father again.

BRIAN. Open it, old boy. There may be a marvellous letter inside.

ALAN. There'll be a letter all right. But I don't need to read it.

He sits down at table and pushes the parcel away.

BRIAN. Bad luck, old boy.

KENNETH *grabs the parcel and unties the string.*

You mustn't give up hope yet, though. First novels are always refused hundreds of times. I know a bloke who's been writing novels and plays and things all his life. He's fifty now, and he's still hoping to get something accepted.

ALAN. Thank you, Brian. That's very comforting.

KENNETH *has extracted a letter from the parcel and is reading it.*

ROGERS. (*Amicably.*) Will you let me read it some time?

ALAN. (*Pleased.*) Would you like to? I'm afraid you'd hate it.

ROGERS. Why? What's it about?

KENNETH *hands down the letter to* ALAN.

ALAN. (*Glancing over letter. He crumples the letter up and throws it away.*) It's about two young men who take a vow to desert their country instantly in the case of war and to go and live on a farm in Central Africa.

ROGERS. (*Uncomfortably.*) Oh.

ALAN. War breaks out and they go. One of them takes his wife. They go, not because they are any more afraid to fight than the next man, but because they believe violence in any circumstances to be a crime and that, if the world goes mad, it's their duty to remain sane.

ROGERS. I see. Conchies.

ALAN. Yes. Conchies. When they get to their farm one of them makes love to the other's wife and they fight over her.

ROGERS. Ah. That's a good point.

ALAN. But in fighting for her they are perfectly aware that the motive that made them do it is as vile as the impulse they feel to go back and fight for their country. In both cases they are letting their passions get the better of their reason – becoming animals instead of men.

ROGERS. But that's nonsense. If a man fights for his country or his wife he's – well, he's a man and not a damned conchie.

ALAN. The characters in my book have the honesty not to rationalise the animal instinct to fight, into something noble like patriotism or manliness. They admit that it's an ignoble instinct – something to be ashamed of.

ROGERS. (*Heated.*) Ashamed of! Crikey!

ALAN. But they also admit that their reason isn't strong enough to stand out against this ignoble instinct, so they go back and fight.

ROGERS. Ah. That's more like it. So they were proved wrong in the end.

ALAN. Their ideal wasn't proved wrong because they were unable to live up to it. That's the point of the book.

KIT. (*From his corner, morosely.*) What's the use of an ideal if you can't live up to it?

ALAN. In a hundred years' time men may be able to live up to our ideals even if they can't live up to their own.

KENNETH. (*Excitedly*.) That's it. Progress.

KIT. Progress my fanny.

ROGERS. But look here, are you a pacifist and all that?

ALAN. I am a pacifist and all that.

ROGERS. And you're going into the diplomatic?

ALAN. Your surprise is a damning criticism of the diplomatic. Anyway, it's not my fault. My father's an ambassador.

ROGERS. Still, I mean to say – Look here, supposing some rotter came along and stole your best girl, wouldn't you fight him?

KIT. (*Looking up*.) You'd better ask me that question, hadn't you?

ROGERS. (*Swinging round*.) What the devil do you mean?

KIT. (*Getting up*.) And the answer would be yes.

ROGERS. (*With heavy sarcasm*.) That's very interesting, I'm sure.

ALAN. (*Enjoying himself*.) By the way, I forgot to tell you, in my novel, when the two men go back to fight for their country they leave the woman in Central Africa. You see after fighting over her they come to the conclusion that she's a bitch. It would have been so much better, don't you think, if they had discovered that sooner?

KIT. All right, you asked for it.

He raises his arm to hit ALAN, *who grapples with him and holds him.*

ALAN. Don't be a damned fool.

ROGERS *strides over and knocks* ALAN *down.*

KIT. (*Turning furiously on* ROGERS.) What the hell do you think you're doing?

KIT *aims a blow at* ROGERS, *who dodges it, overturning a chair.* KENNETH *runs in to attack* ROGERS. BRIAN, *also running in, tries to restrain both* KENNETH *and* KIT.

BRIAN. Shut up, you damned lot of fools. (*Shouting*.) Kit, Babe, show some sense, for God's sake! Look out – Maingot!

ALAN *gets up and is about to go for* ROGERS *when* MAINGOT *comes in from the garden, carrying a large notebook under his arm.* KIT, KENNETH, *and* BRIAN *sit down.* ROGERS *and* ALAN *stand glaring at each other.* MAINGOT *picks up the chair that has been knocked over, pulls it to the table, sits down, and spreads his notebook out on the table.*

MAINGOT. Alors, asseyez-vous, Messieurs. Le sujet cet après-midi sera la crise de mille huit cent quarante en Turquie.

ALAN and ROGERS *sit down, still glaring at each other.*

Or la dernière fois je vous ai expliqué comment le gouverneur ottoman d'Egypte, Mehemet Ali, s'était battu contre son souverain, le Sultan de Turquie. Constatons donc que la chute du Sultanat . . .

Curtain.

Act Two, Scene Two

Scene: the same. Time: about six hours later.

DIANA *is discovered sitting in one armchair, her feet up on the other. She is smoking a cigarette and gazing listlessly out of the window.*

JACQUELINE *comes in through door at back, dressed in a Bavarian costume.*

JACQUELINE. Hullo! Aren't you getting dressed?

DIANA. (*Turning her head. She gets up and examines* JACQUELINE.) Darling, you look too lovely.

JACQUELINE. Do you like it?

DIANA. I adore it. I think it's sweet. (*She continues her examination.*) If I were you, dear, I'd wear that hat just a little more on the back of the head. Look, I'll show you. (*She arranges* JACQUELINE*'s hat.*) No, that's not quite right. I wonder if it'd look better without a hat at all. (*She removes hat.*) No, you must wear a hat.

JACQUELINE. I suppose my hair's wrong.

DIANA. Well, it isn't quite Bavarian, is it, darling? Very nice, of course. (*Pulling* JACQUELINE*'s dress about.*) There's something wrong here. (*She kneels down and begins to rearrange the dress.*)

Pause.

JACQUELINE. I've got something to say to you, Diana. Do you mind if I say it now?

DIANA. Of course not. (*Tugging dress.*) Oh, lord, there's a bit of braid coming off here.

JACQUELINE. Oh!

DIANA. I'll fix it for you.

JACQUELINE. If you look in that basket over there you'll find a needle and thread. (*She points to a work-basket which is lying on the seat of one of the chairs.*)

DIANA. Right. (*She goes to basket.*)

JACQUELINE. But you needn't trouble –

DIANA. (*Extracting needle and thread.*) That's all right. It's no trouble. I enjoy doing this sort of thing. (*Threading needle.*) Well, what was it you wanted to say to me?

JACQUELINE. I overheard your conversation with the Commander this afternoon.

DIANA. (*Making a bad shot with the thread. She turns to the light.*) All of it, or just a part of it?

JACQUELINE. I heard you say that you were in love with the Commander and that you didn't love Kit.

DIANA. Oh! (*Kneeling at* JACQUELINE*'s feet.*) Now, scream if I stick a needle into you, won't you? (*She begins to sew.*) Is that what you wanted to tell me?

JACQUELINE. I wanted to know if you were going to tell Kit that you didn't love him.

DIANA. (*Sewing industriously.*) Why?

JACQUELINE. Because if you don't tell him, I will.

DIANA. (*After a slight pause.*) My poor Jacqueline, I never knew you felt like that about Kit.

JACQUELINE. Yes, you did. You've known for some time, and you've had a lot of fun out of it.

DIANA. Well, I wish you the best of luck.

JACQUELINE. Thank you. (*Starting.*) Ow!

DIANA. Sorry, darling, did I prick you?

JACQUELINE. Are you going to tell him?

DIANA. I don't think so.

JACQUELINE. I shall, then.

DIANA. My dear, I think that would be very silly. He won't believe you, it'll make him very unhappy, and, worst of all, he'll be furious with you.

JACQUELINE. (*Thoughtfully*.) Yes, that's true, I suppose.

DIANA. (*Biting off the thread and standing up*.) There. How's that?

JACQUELINE. Thank you so much. That's splendid. So you won't leave Kit alone?

DIANA. Now, let's be honest, for a moment. Don't let's talk about love and things like that, but just plain facts. You and I both want the same man.

JACQUELINE. But you don't –

DIANA. Oh yes, I do.

JACQUELINE. But what about the Commander?

DIANA. I want him too.

JACQUELINE. Oh!

DIANA. Don't look shocked, darling. You see, I'm not like you. You're clever – you can talk intelligently, and you're nice.

JACQUELINE. That's a horrid word.

DIANA. Now I'm not nice. I'm not clever and I can't talk intelligently. There's only one thing I've got, and I don't think you'll deny it. I have got a sort of gift for making men fall in love with me.

JACQUELINE. Oh, no. I don't deny that at all.

DIANA. Thank you, darling. I didn't think you would. Well, now, you have been sent into the world with lots of gifts, and you make use of them. Well, what about me, with just my one gift? I must use that too, mustn't I?

JACQUELINE. Well, what you call my gifts are at any rate social. Yours are definitely anti-social.

DIANA. Oh, I can't be bothered with all that. The fact remains that having men in love with me is my whole life. It's hard for you to understand, I know. You see, you're the sort of person that people *like*. But nobody *likes* me.

JACQUELINE. Oh, I wish you wouldn't keep harping on that. I wouldn't mind if everybody hated me, provided Kit loved me.

DIANA. You can't have it both ways, darling. Kit looks on you as a very nice person.

JACQUELINE. (*With sudden anger*.) Oh, God! What I'd give to be anything but nice!

DIANA. In a way, you know, I envy you. It must be very pleasant to be able to make friends with people.

JACQUELINE. You could be friends with Kit if you were honest with him.

DIANA. Darling! And I called you intelligent! Kit despises me. If he didn't love me he'd loathe me. That's why I can't let him go.

JACQUELINE. (*Pleadingly.*) Oh, Diana, I do see your point of view. I do see that you must have men in love with you, but couldn't you, please, couldn't you make the Commander do?

DIANA. No – I always act on the principle that there's safety in numbers.

JACQUELINE. Well, there's this Lord Heybrook arriving tomorrow. Supposing I let you have the Commander and him.

DIANA. No, darling. I'm sorry. I'd do anything else for you, but if you want Kit, you must win him in fair fight.

JACQUELINE. (*A shade tearfully.*) But I don't stand a chance against you.

DIANA. To be perfectly honest, I agree with you, darling.

JACQUELINE. I only hope you make some awful blunder, so that he finds out the game you're playing.

DIANA. (*With dignity.*) I don't make blunders. He's taking you to the Casino tonight, isn't he?

JACQUELINE. Yes, but he's so furious because you're going with the Commander that he'll give me the most dreadful evening.

DIANA. That's all right. I'm not going. I don't feel like it, as a matter of fact.

JACQUELINE. But have you told the Commander?

DIANA. Yes; he's furious, poor poppet, but it's very good for him.

JACQUELINE. (*After a pause.*) I wonder if you realise the trouble you cause? You know there was a fight about you this afternoon?

DIANA. Yes. I hear Alan was in it. That's *very* interesting.

JACQUELINE *is surprised.* DIANA *smiles.* KIT's *voice is heard off, calling 'Jack, where are you?'* JACQUELINE *turns to* DIANA *in sudden fright.*

JACQUELINE. Does Kit know you're not going tonight?

KIT *comes in through door at back. His lower half is enclosed in the frilly skirt of a Greek Evzone, beneath which can be seen an ordinary pair of socks with suspenders. In addition he wears a cricket shirt and tie. He carries the tunic over his arm.*

KIT. Jack, I can't get into this damned coat.

DIANA *bursts into a shriek of laughter.*

DIANA. Kit, you look angelic! I wish you could see yourself.

KIT. You shut up.

JACQUELINE. I told you it might be rather a tight fit.

KIT. But it's miles too small. Your brother must be a pygmy.

JACQUELINE. Take that shirt off and then try.

KIT. Jack, would you mind terribly if I didn't come? I can't go dressed as an inebriated danseuse.

DIANA *shrieks with laughter again.*

JACQUELINE. Don't be silly, Kit. It's going to look lovely.

KIT. Honestly, though, I don't think I'll come. You wouldn't mind?

JACQUELINE. I'd mind – awfully.

KIT. Alan's not going. I don't think I can face it really. I've asked Babe if he'll take you, and he says he'd love to. (*Turning to* DIANA – *off-handedly.*) I hear you're not going, Diana.

DIANA. No. I feel rather like you about it.

KIT. (*To* DIANA.) You know, they have dancing in the streets tonight. We might get rid of the others later and go out and join in the general whoopee – what do you say?

DIANA. Yes, that's a lovely idea, Kit.

KIT. (*Turning to* JACQUELINE.) I'm awfully sorry, Jack, but honestly –

JACQUELINE. It's all right. I'll have a lovely time with Kenneth. (*She goes out quickly through door at back.*)

KIT. She seems rather odd. You don't think she minds, do you?

DIANA. Well, how on earth should I know?

KIT. Darling, if we go out tonight, you will get rid of the Commander, won't you? If he comes I won't be answerable for the consequences.

DIANA. He's not so easy to get rid of. He clings like a limpet. Still, I'll do my best.

KIT. I can't understand why you don't just tell him to go to hell.

DIANA. (*Gently.*) That'd be a little – cruel, wouldn't it, Kit?

KIT. As someone said once, why not be cruel only to be kind?

DIANA. Yes, that's true, but, you know, Kit, cruelty is something that's physically impossible to me. I'm the sort of person who's miserable if I tread on a snail.

KIT. But can't you see, darling? It's unfair on him to let him go on thinking he's got a hope.

DIANA. Poor old Bill. Oh, well, darling, come and give me a kiss and say you love me.

ROGERS *comes in through garden door.*

KIT. With pleasure. (*He kisses her, although she tries to push him away.*) I love you.

ROGERS. (*To* KIT.) What the devil do you think you're doing?

KIT. I'll give you three guesses.

ROGERS. I've had enough of this. I'm going to give this young puppy a good hiding.

DIANA. (*Trying to separate them.*) Don't be silly, Bill.

ROGERS. Out of the way, Diana.

KIT. Do what the Commander says, Diana.

DIANA. (*Still separating them.*) You're both quite mad.

MAINGOT *comes in through door at back dressed in Scottish Highland costume.* BRIAN *and* ALAN *follow, gazing at him with rapture.* KIT *and* ROGERS *and* DIANA *break apart.*

ALAN. (*Clasping his hands in admiration.*) Mais c'est exquis, Monsieur! Parfait!

MAINGOT. N'est-ce pas que c'est beau? Je l'ai choisi moi-même. Ça me va bien, hein?

ALAN. C'est tout ce qu'il y a de plus chic.

BRIAN. Vous ne pouvez pas dire le différence entre vous et un réel Highlander.

MAINGOT. Mais oui. Ça – c'est un véritable costume écossais.

DIANA. Oh, yes, that is formidable.

MAINGOT. (*Crossing to* DIANA) Vous croyez? Et aussi je connais quelques pas du can-can écossais.

ALAN. Amusez-vous bien, Monsieur.

MAINGOT. Merci.

BRIAN. J'espère que vous baiserez beaucoup de dames, Monsieur.

MAINGOT. (*Turning appalled.*) Ha? Qu'est qu'il dit, ce garçon la?

BRIAN. Ai-je dit quelque chose?

MAINGOT. Une bétise, Monsieur. On ne dit jamais baiser – embrasser. Il ne faut pas me donner des idées.

He goes out chuckling. ALAN, BRIAN, *and* DIANA *go to the window to watch him go down the street.* KIT *and* ROGERS *stand looking at each other rather sheepishly.*

ALAN. My God! What *does* he look like?

DIANA. He looks perfectly sweet.

JACQUELINE *comes in, followed by* KENNETH, *in sailor costume.*

BRIAN. Your father's just gone off, Jack. If you hurry you can catch him.

JACQUELINE. Right. (*Gaily.*) Goodbye, everyone. You're all fools not to be coming. We're going to have a lovely time.

KENNETH. (*To* ALAN.) Alan, do change your mind and come.

ALAN. No, thank you, Babe – have a good time.

KENNETH. Alan –

ALAN. Well, I'm going to have a drink. Anyone coming with me?

BRIAN. I'm ahead of you, old boy.

DIANA. Yes, I'm coming.

ALAN. I suppose that means I'll have to pay for both of you.

DIANA. Yes, it does.

ALAN. Are you two coming?

ROGERS *and* KIT *look at each other and then shake their heads.*

ROGERS AND KIT. No.

DIANA *and* BRIAN, KENNETH *and* JACQUELINE *all go out, talking.*

ALAN. Oh, no. I see you're going to have a musical evening! (*He follows the other two out.*)

KIT. Now we can have our little talk.

ROGERS. I don't mean to do much talking.

KIT. But I do. Diana has just this minute given me a message to give you. She wants you to understand that she knows what you feel about her, and she's sorry for you. But she must ask you not to take advantage of her pity for you to make her life a burden.

ROGERS. Right. Now that you've had your joke, let me tell you the truth. This afternoon Diana asked me to let you know, in as kindly a way as possible, that her feelings for you have changed entirely, and that she is now in love with me.

KIT. (*Astounded*.) God! What nerve! Do you know what she's just said about you? (*Shouting*.) She called you a silly old bore, who stuck like a limpet and weren't worth bothering about.

ROGERS. Oh, she did, did she?

KIT. Yes, she did, and a lot more besides that wouldn't bear repeating.

ROGERS. All right, you lying young fool. I've felt sorry for you up to this, but now I see I've got to teach you a lesson. Put your hands up.

KIT. (*Putting up his fists*.) It's a pleasure.

They stand facing each other, ready for battle. Pause.
ROGERS *suddenly begins to laugh.*

ROGERS. (*Collapsing, doubled up with laughter, into a chair*.) You look so damned funny in that get-up.

KIT. (*Looking down at his legs, and beginning to giggle*.) A little eccentric, I admit.

ROGERS. Like a bedraggled old fairy queen.

KIT. I'll go and change.

ROGERS. (*Becoming serious*.) No, don't. If you do I'll have to fight you. I can't when you're looking like that, and if you go on looking like that it'll save us from making idiots of ourselves.

KIT. You know, that's rather sensible. I am surprised.

ROGERS. You know, I'm not quite such a damned fool as you youngsters seem to think. As a matter of fact, I'm a perfectly rational being, and I'm prepared to discuss this particular situation rationally. Now, I'm ready to admit that you have a grievance against me.

KIT. But I haven't – speaking rationally.

ROGERS. Oh, yes. Rationally speaking, you might say that I've alienated the affections of your sweetheart.

KIT. (*Smiling*.) But you haven't done anything of the sort.

ROGERS. (*Raising his hand*.) Please don't interrupt. Now, I'm perfectly ready to apologise for something that isn't altogether my fault. I hope you will accept it in the spirit in which it is offered.

KIT. (*Incredulous*.) But do you really think Diana's in love with you?

ROGERS. Certainly.

KIT. Why do you think that?

ROGERS. She told me so, of course.

KIT. (*Laughing.*) My poor, dear Commander –

ROGERS. I thought we were going to discuss this matter rationally?

KIT. Yes, but when you begin with a flagrant misrepresentation of the facts –

ROGERS. You mean, I'm a liar?

KIT. Yes, that's exactly what I do mean.

ROGERS. (*Jumping to his feet.*) Come on. Get up. I see I've got to fight you, skirt or no skirt.

KIT. No, no. Let reason have one last fling. If that fails we can give way to our animal passions. Let me tell you my side of the case.

ROGERS. (*Sitting.*) All right.

KIT. I've just had a talk with Diana. She said you were in love with her. I suggested to her that it was only fair to you to let you know exactly where you stood – in other words, that she was in love with me and that you had no chance. She answered that, though what I'd said was the truth –

ROGERS. She never said that.

KIT. (*Raising his hand.*) Please don't interrupt. (*Continuing.*) Though what I'd said was the truth, she couldn't tell you because it would be too cruel.

ROGERS *starts slightly.*

I then said, rather aptly, that this was a case where she should be cruel only to be kind.

ROGERS. You said what?

KIT. Cruel only to be kind.

ROGERS. What did she say?

KIT. She said she found it physically impossible to be cruel. She said she was the sort of person who was miserable if she trod on a snail.

ROGERS. What? You're sure of that?

KIT. Certainly.

ROGERS. She said she was miserable if she trod on a snail?

KIT. Yes.

ROGERS. (*With a world of feeling.*) Good God!

KIT. What's the matter?

ROGERS. It's awful! (*Rising and walking about.*) I can't believe it. I don't believe it. This is all a monstrous plot. (*Swinging round.*) I believe you listened in to my conversation with Diana this afternoon.

KIT. Why?

ROGERS. Because I also told her she ought to be cruel only to be kind, and she made precisely the same answer as she made to you.

KIT. (*After a pause.*) You mean about the snail?

ROGERS. Yes, about the snail.

KIT. In other words she's been double-crossing us. No, you've made all that up.

ROGERS. I only wish I had.

KIT. How do I know you're telling the truth?

ROGERS. You'll have to take my word for it.

KIT. Why should I?

ROGERS. Do you want to make me fight you?

KIT. Yes, I do.

Pause.

ROGERS. Well, I'm not going to.

KIT. (*Sitting down suddenly.*) I wonder why it's such a comfort to get away from reason.

ROGERS. Because in this case reason tells us something our vanity won't let us accept.

KIT. It tells us that Diana's a bitch.

ROGERS *half moves out of his chair.*

Reason! Reason!

ROGERS *subsides.*

ROGERS. You're right. We'd better face it. Diana's in love with neither of us, and she's made a fool out of both of us.

KIT. We don't know that – I mean that she's in love with neither of us. She may be telling lies to one and the truth to the other.

ROGERS. Is that what your reason tells you?

KIT. No.

Pause. They are both sunk in gloom.

I feel rather sick.

ROGERS. I must have a stronger stomach than you.

Pause.

I suppose you loved her more than I did?

KIT. Loved her? I still do love her, damn it.

ROGERS. But you can't, now that you know what you do.

KIT. What difference does that make? I love her face, I love the way she walks, I love her voice, I love her figure. None of that has changed.

ROGERS. (*Sympathetically.*) Poor boy. It's simpler for me though it's far more of a shock. You see, what I loved about her was her character.

Pause.

KIT. You used to kiss her, I suppose?

ROGERS. (*Sadly.*) Oh, yes.

KIT. You didn't – you didn't – ?

ROGERS. (*Severely.*) I loved her for her character. (*After a pause.*) Did you?

KIT. Well, no, not really.

ROGERS. I see.

Pause.

KIT. What are we going to do?

ROGERS. We'd better face her together. We'll ask her point-blank which of us she really does love.

KIT. If she says me, I'm done for.

ROGERS. But you won't believe her?

KIT. I'll know she's lying, but I'll believe her all the same.

ROGERS. Well, supposing she says me?

KIT. That's my only hope.

ROGERS. Then, for your sake, I hope she says me.

KIT. That's terribly kind of you, Bill. I say, I may call you Bill, mayn't I?

ROGERS. Oh, my dear Kit.

Pause.

You know, what I feel like doing is to go out and get very drunk.

KIT. Suppose we go and throw ourselves into the sea instead.

ROGERS. I think my idea is better.

KIT. Yes, perhaps you're right. Then let's start now.

ROGERS. You can't go out like that, my dear Kit.

KIT. Then let's go to the Casino.

ROGERS. I haven't got anything to wear.

KIT. (*Holding out tunic.*) Wear this over your flannels.

ROGERS. All right. Help me put it on.

ALAN *and* BRIAN *come in.* KIT *is buttoning up* ROGERS' *tunic. They both stop in amazement.*

ALAN. What on earth – ?

KIT. (*Excitedly.*) Bill and I are going to the Casino, Alan. You've got to come, too.

ALAN. Bill and you? What is this? Some new sort of game?

KIT. Go and put something on. You come, too, Brian.

BRIAN. No, old boy. Not me.

KIT. Go on, Alan. We want to get out of the house before Diana arrives. Where is she, by the way?

ROGERS. Who cares!

KIT *laughs.*

ALAN. (*Scratching his head.*) Let me get this straight. You want me to come to the Ball with you and the Commander –

KIT. Don't call him the Commander, Alan. His name is Bill.

ALAN. Bill?

KIT. Yes, Bill. He's one of the best fellows in the world.

ROGERS. We're going to get drunk together, aren't we, Kit?

ALAN. Kit?

KIT. Screaming drunk, Bill.

ALAN. (*Dashing to door.*) I won't be a minute.

Exit ALAN.

BRIAN. This sounds like a party.

KIT. Brian, tell me how I can get hold of your Chi-Chi? Is she going to the Casino tonight?

BRIAN. Yes, old boy.

KIT. How can I recognise her?

BRIAN. I don't think you can miss her. She's not likely to miss you, anyway, if you go into the bar alone.

KIT. Has she got a good figure?

BRIAN. I like it, but I'm easy to please. From sideways on it's a bit S-shaped, if you know what I mean.

ALAN comes down, wearing his German coat.

ALAN. I shall probably be lynched in this thing.

KIT. Come on. Let's go.

They go to the window. KIT *with his arm across* ROGERS' *shoulder.*

BRIAN. Hi! Wait a minute. What am I to tell Diana?

They stop.

ROGERS. Tell her we're being cruel only to be kind.

KIT. Tell her to be careful she doesn't go treading on any snails.

ALAN. Just tell her to go to hell. That leaves no room for doubt.

They go out. BRIAN *gazes after them as the curtain falls.*

Act Three, Scene One

Scene: the same. Time: A few hours later.

The curtain rises to disclose ALAN *on the sofa,* KIT *in the armchair,* ROGERS *on the floor by the end of the sofa, each smoking a cigar. They are still in the clothes in which they had gone to the Casino.* ROGERS *is half asleep.*

KIT. (*Drowsily.*) I don't agree with you. I don't agree with you at all. You can't judge women by our standards of Right and Wrong.

ALAN. They have none of their own, so how can you judge them.

KIT. Why judge them at all. There they are – all of them, I grant you, behaving absolutely nohow – still, that's what they're for, I mean they're built that way, and you've just got to take them or leave them. I'll take them.

ROGERS. (*Murmuring dreamily.*) I'll take vanilla.

KIT. Now, you tell me that Diana's a cow. All right, I shan't deny it. I shall only say that I, personally, like cows.

ALAN. But you can like them without loving them. I mean, love is only sublimated sex, isn't it?

ROGERS. (*Rousing himself a little.*) Devilish funny thing – my old friend Freud, the last time I met him, said exactly the same thing. Bill, old man, he said, take my word for it, love is only sublimated sex. (*Composing himself for sleep again.*) That's what Old Freudie said.

ALAN. I fear that Bill is what he'd describe himself as half seas over.

KIT. He's lucky. The more I drank up at that foul Casino the more sober I became. What were you saying about sublimated sex?

ALAN. Only that if that's what you feel for Diana, why sublimate?

KIT. Ah! Because she's clever enough to give me no choice.

ALAN. How simple everything would be if that sort of so-called virtue were made illegal – if it were just a question of will you or won't you.

ROGERS' *head falls back on to the chair.*

No one ought to be allowed to get away with that – 'I'd like to but I mustn't'. It's that that leads to all the trouble. The Commander has now definitely passed out. You know (*excitedly*) I like him, Kit. It's quite amazing how pleasant he is when you get to know him.

A slight smile appears on ROGERS' *face*.

KIT. Yes, I know.

ALAN. Do you realise that if it hadn't been for Diana, we'd probably have gone on disliking him for ever?

KIT. Yes. We've got to be grateful to her for that.

ALAN. I wonder why we disliked him so much before tonight.

ROGERS. (*From a horizontal position.*) I'll tell you.

ALAN. Good lord! I thought you'd passed out.

ROGERS. Officers in the Royal Navy never pass out.

ALAN. They just fall on the floor in an alcoholic stupor, I suppose?

ROGERS. Exactly.

KIT. Well, tell us why we disliked you so much.

ROGERS. Right.

ALAN *helps him to a sitting position*.

Because you all made up your mind to dislike me before I ever came into this house. All except Diana, that's to say. From the moment I arrived, you all treated me as if I were some interesting old relic of a bygone age. I've never known such an unfriendly lot of blighters as you all were.

ALAN. We thought you were a bumptious bore.

ROGERS. Oh, I may have seemed a bortious bump, but that was only because I was in a blue funk of you all. Here was I who'd never been away from my ship for more than a few days at a time, suddenly plumped down in a house full of strange people, all talking either French, which I couldn't understand, or your own brand of English, which was almost as hard, and all convinced I was a half-wit. Of course I was in a blue funk.

ALAN. Well, I'm damned.

ROGERS. As a matter of fact, I liked you all.

ALAN. Oh, that's very gratifying.

ROGERS. I didn't agree with most of your opinions, but I enjoyed listening to them. I wanted to discuss them with you, but I was never given the chance. You all seemed to think that because I was in the Navy I was incapable of consecutive thought – I say, whisky doesn't half loosen the old tongue.

ALAN. But you always seemed so aggressive.

ROGERS. I was only defending myself. You attacked first, you know.

ALAN. (*Contritely.*) I'm terribly sorry.

ROGERS. That's all right. As a matter of fact it's done me a lot of good being here. One gets into a bit of a rut, you know, in the Service. One's apt to forget that there are some people in the world who have different ideas and opinions to one's own. You'll find the same in the diplomatic.

ALAN. I know. That's one of the reasons I want to chuck it.

ROGERS. Will you let me give you a bit of advice about that? I've been wanting to for a long time, but I've always been afraid you'd bite my head off if I did.

ALAN. Of course.

ROGERS. Well, chuck it. Go and do your writing.

ALAN *looks surprised. He takes a deep puff at his cigar.*

ALAN. I'd go back to England tomorrow, only – (*He stops.*)

ROGERS. Only what?

ALAN. I don't know if I can write, for one thing.

ROGERS. It's ten to one you can't, but I shouldn't let that stop you. If it's what you want to do, I should do it.

ALAN. That isn't the real reason.

ROGERS. You haven't got the guts, is that it?

ALAN. That isn't quite my way of putting it, but I suppose it's true. I can't bring myself to make a definite decision. I'm afraid of my father, of course. But it's not only that. I admit that there are a dozen things I'd rather do than the diplomatic. It's an exciting world at the moment. Do you know, sometimes I think I'll go and fight. There must be a war on somewhere.

ROGERS. I thought you were a pacifist?

ALAN. Oh, what the hell? – I shall become a diplomat.

ROGERS. You'll be a damned bad one.

ALAN. I can adapt myself.

ROGERS. (*Rising, yawning.*) Well, I've given you my advice for what it's worth. I shall now go to bed to sleep the sleep of the very drunk.

ALAN. You mustn't go yet. You've got to wait for Diana.

ROGERS. (*With a magnificent gesture.*) Diana – pooh!

ALAN. It's all very well for you to say 'Diana – pooh', but this weak-kneed, jelly-livered protoplasm here is still in her clutches.

KIT. (*Who has been musing.*) Are you referring to me?

ALAN. Diana's only got to raise her little finger and he'll go rushing back to her, screaming to be forgiven.

ROGERS. Then we must stop her raising her little finger.

ALAN. Exactly. That's why we must face her together.

ROGERS. (*Sitting heavily.*) The United Front. We must scupper her with a plunging salvo.

ALAN. Oh, no, don't let's do that.

KIT. (*Dismally.*) She's only got to say she still loves me.

ALAN. My dear Kit, if she has to choose between you and Bill, she'll choose you. You're younger, you're better-looking, and you've got more money. Don't you agree, Bill?

ROGERS. He's certainly younger and he's certainly got more money.

ALAN. (*To* KIT.) You must be firm, you must be strong. If you show any weakness, you'll be a traitor to our sex.

ROGERS. By jove, yes. We must put up a good show in this engagement.

KIT. It's all very well for you to talk. You don't know –

ALAN. Haven't I resisted her attacks for a whole month?

KIT. They were only little skirmishes. You don't know what it is to receive the whole brunt of her attack. It's quite hopeless. You can help me as much as you like, but if she attacks me directly, I shall go under, I know that.

ALAN. Do you hear that, Commander? I submit that he be tried for Extreme Cowardice in the face of the Enemy.

ROGERS. The Court finds the prisoner guilty. (*Rising with dignity.*) Mr. Neilan, I must call upon you to surrender your trousers. Ah? I see you have come into court without them. Very well, I have no option but to ask you for your skirt.

KIT. Come and get it.

ROGERS. I've been longing to get my hands on that damn thing all the evening. Come on, Alan.

KIT *leaps out of his chair, and runs across the room pursued by* ROGERS *and* ALAN. *He is cornered and there is a scuffle.* DIANA, *stately and sad, comes through the French windows.*

She stands in the doorway for some five seconds before
ROGERS *sees her.*

ROGERS. Crikey! (*He taps the two others on the shoulders and they straighten themselves.*)

There is a rather nervous silence.

DIANA. (*Coming into the room.*) Well – I hope you all enjoyed yourselves at the Casino.

ROGERS. (*After glancing at the others.*) Oh, yes. Thanks very much.

DIANA. Brian gave me a message from you which I found rather hard to understand. Perhaps you'd explain it now.

Pause. ALAN *looks inquiringly from* KIT *to* ROGERS. ROGERS *looks appealingly at* ALAN.

ALAN. Well, who is to fire the first shot of the salvo?

No answer.

Come, come, gentlemen.

No answer.

Very well, I must engage the enemy on your behalf. Diana, these two gentlemen have good reason to believe that you have been trifling with their affections. You have told Kit that you are in love with him and are bored by Bill, and you have told Bill that you are in love with him and are bored by Kit. So now they naturally want to know who exactly you are in love with and who exactly you are bored by.

ROGERS. (*Nodding vigorously.*) Yes, that's right.

DIANA. (*With scorn.*) Oh, do they?

ALAN. Are you going to answer their question?

DIANA. Certainly not. Whom I love and whom I don't love is entirely my own affair. I've never heard such insolence.

ALAN. (*Turning to* ROGERS *and* KIT, *chuckling.*) Insolence! She's good, this girl, she's very good.

DIANA. (*Patiently.*) May I please be allowed to go to my room?

ALAN. (*Barring her way.*) Not until you've answered our question.

DIANA. I think you'd better let me go.

ALAN. Just as soon as you've given a straight answer to a straight question.

Pause. DIANA *at length takes a step back.*

DIANA. All right. You want to know who I'm in love with. Well, I'll tell you. (*To* ALAN.) I'm in love with you.

ALAN *recoils. There is a dead silence.*

DIANA *brushes past* ALAN. *He seizes her wrist.*

DIANA. Good night!

ALAN *drops his hands and steps back. He falls limply into a chair.* DIANA *goes out.*

ROGERS. (*Scratching his head.*) Now will someone tell me, was our engagement a success?

ALAN. (*Bitterly.*) A success? (*Groaning.*) Oh, what a girl, what a girl!

KIT. (*Gloomily.*) It was a success as far as I'm concerned.

Pause.

ALAN. I'm frightened. I'm really frightened.

ROGERS. What? (*Sternly.*) Alan, I never thought to hear such words from you.

ALAN. I can't help it. I shall fall. Oh, God! I know it, I shall fall.

ROGERS. You must be firm. You must be strong. The United Front must not be broken.

ALAN. I want you to promise me something, you two. You must never, never leave me alone with that girl.

ROGERS. That sounds like rank cowardice.

ALAN. Cowardice be damned! You don't realise the appalling danger I'm in. If I'm left alone with her for a minute, I shudder to think what might happen. She might even (*in a whisper*) marry me.

ROGERS. Oh, not that.

ALAN. It's true. God help me. I think she may easily try to marry me. (*Turning imploringly to the others.*) So you see, you can't desert me now. Don't let me out of your sight for a second. Even if I beg you on my knees to leave me alone with her, don't do it. Will you promise?

ROGERS. I promise.

ALAN. And you, Kit?

KIT. (*Nods.*) All right.

ALAN. Thank you. I've only got three weeks before the exam, but that's a long time with Diana in the house.

ROGERS. I think your hope lies in this Lord Heybrook fellow who's coming tomorrow. She may easily find that a peer in hand is worth more than one in the vague future. (*Getting up.*) I shall go to bed. Good night, Alan. You have my best wishes. (*At door.*) Don't go down to breakfast tomorrow until I come and fetch you. Good night, Kit. (*He goes out.*)

ALAN. There's a real friend. I hope you're going to show the same self-sacrifice.

KIT. I don't know what you're making all the fuss about. You ought to be very happy.

ALAN. Happy? (*Sarcastically.*) I've noticed how happy you've been these last few weeks.

KIT. I have in a way.

ALAN. That's not my way. Damn it, Kit, I'm a man with principles and ideals. I'm a romantic. Let me give you a little word-picture of the girl I should like to fall in love with. Then you can tell how far it resembles Diana. First of all, she must not be a cow.

KIT. (*Shrugging indifferently.*) Oh, well, of course –

ALAN. Secondly, she will be able to converse freely and intelligently with me on all subjects – Politics – Philosophy – Religion – Thirdly, she will have all the masculine virtues and none of the feminine vices. Fourthly, she will be physically unattractive enough to keep her faithful to me, and attractive enough to make me desire her. Fifthly, she will be in love with me. That's all, I think.

KIT. You don't want much, do you? I admit it isn't a close description of Diana, but where on earth do you expect to find this love-dream?

ALAN. They do exist, you know. There's someone here, in this house, who answers to all the qualifications, except the last.

KIT. (*Sitting forward.*) Good lord! You don't mean Jack, do you?

ALAN. Why not?

KIT. But – but you couldn't be in love with Jack.

ALAN. I'm not, but she's exactly the sort of girl I should like to be in love with.

KIT. (*Smiling.*) Love and Jack. They just don't seem to connect. I'm frightfully fond of her, but somehow – I don't know – I mean you couldn't kiss her or make love to her.

ALAN. Why not try it and see?

KIT. Who? Me? Good lord, no.

ALAN. Don't you think she's attractive?

KIT. Yes, I suppose she is, in a way, very attractive. But don't you see, Alan, I know her far too well to start any hanky-panky. She'd just scream with laughter.

ALAN. Really? She'd just scream with laughter? (*Turning on him.*) You poor idiot, don't you realise the girl's been madly in love with you for two months now?

KIT. (*After a pause, derisively.*) Ha, ha!

ALAN. All right. Say ha, ha! Don't believe it and forget I ever said it. I promised her I'd never tell you.

Pause.

KIT. What did you have to drink up at the Casino?

ALAN. Less than you.

KIT. Are you stone-cold sober?

ALAN. As sober as ten Lady Astors.

KIT. And you sit there and tell me –

Voices heard outside.

(*Getting up in alarm.*) Oh, lord!

MAINGOT *comes in, followed by* JACQUELINE *and* KENNETH.

MAINGOT. Aha! Le Grec et l'Allemand. Vous vous êtes bien amusés au Casino?

JACQUELINE. Hello, Kit.

ALAN. Très bien, Monsieur. Et vous?

KIT *is gaping open-mouthed at* JACQUELINE.

MAINGOT. Ah, oui! C'était assez gai, mais on y a mangé excessivement mal, et le champagne était très mauvais et m'a couté les yeux de la tête. Quand même le quartorze ne vient qu'une fois par an. Alors je vais me coucher. Bonsoir, bonne nuit et dormez bien.

ALL. Bonsoir.

MAINGOT *goes out through door at back, carrying his Highland shoes which he has changed for slippers.*

JACQUELINE. Why did you all leave so early?

KIT. (*Gaping.*) Oh, I don't know.

JACQUELINE. Your costume caused a sensation, Kit. Everyone was asking me what it was meant to be.

KIT. (*Nervously*.) Really.

ALAN. Did you have a good time, Kenneth?

KENNETH. Oh, all right. I'll say good night. I've got an essay to finish before tomorrow.

JACQUELINE. Good night, Kenneth, and thank you.

KENNETH. Good night.

> KENNETH *goes out, looking sulky, through door at back.*

ALAN. You must have had a wonderful time with the Babe in that mood.

JACQUELINE. What's the matter with him, Alan?

ALAN. He's angry with me for not doing his essay for him. I think I'd better go and make my peace with him. (*At door.*) Don't go to bed for a few minutes. I want to talk to you, Jack.

> *He goes out. There is a pause.* KIT *is plainly uncomfortable.*

KIT. Jack?

JACQUELINE. Yes?

KIT. Did you have a good time tonight?

JACQUELINE. (*Puzzled*.) Yes, thank you, Kit.

KIT. Good. I – er – I'm sorry I couldn't take you.

JACQUELINE. That's all right. (*Smiling*.) That was Brian's girl you and Alan were dancing with, wasn't it? What's she like?

KIT. Pretty hellish.

> *Pause.*

> Jack?

JACQUELINE. Yes?

KIT. Oh, nothing. (*He gets up and wanders forlornly about the room.*) Was it raining when you came back?

JACQUELINE. No, it wasn't raining.

KIT. It was when we came back.

JACQUELINE. Really?

> *Pause.*

KIT. Yes, quite heavily.

JACQUELINE. It must have cleared up, then.

> *Pause.* KIT *is fiddling with a box of matches.*

KIT. (*Turning with sudden decision*.) Jack, there's something I must – (*In turning he upsets matches.*) Damn, I'm sorry.

JACQUELINE. I've never seen a clumsier idiot than you, Kit. (*She goes on her knees.*) I seem to spend my life cleaning up after you. There!

She gets up. KIT *kisses her suddenly and clumsily on the mouth. She pushes him away. They are both embarrassed and puzzled.*

(*After a long pause.*) You smell of whisky, Kit.

Enter ALAN.

ALAN. Oh!

KIT. I'm going to bed. Good night. (*He goes out.*)

JACQUELINE. What's the matter with him? Is he drunk?

ALAN. No, Jack, but I've a confession to make to you.

JACQUELINE. (*In alarm.*) You haven't told him?

ALAN. I couldn't help it.

JACQUELINE. Oh, Alan, no.

ALAN. Will you forgive me?

JACQUELINE. I'll never forgive you. It's ruined everything. (*A shade tearfully.*) He's just been talking to me about the weather.

ALAN. Well, he's a bit embarrassed. That's natural.

JACQUELINE. But he'll spend all his time running away from me now, and when he is with me he'll always be wondering if I want him to kiss me, and he'll go on talking about the weather, and – (*turning away*) – oh, it's awful!

ALAN. I'm sorry, Jack. I meant well.

JACQUELINE. Men are such blundering fools.

ALAN. Yes, I suppose we are. Will you forgive me?

JACQUELINE. (*Wearily.*) Of course I forgive you. (*After a pause.*) I'm going to bed.

ALAN. All right. We'll talk about it in the morning. I may be able to persuade Kit I was joking.

JACQUELINE. (*At door.*) No. Please don't say anything more to Kit. You've done enough harm as it is. (*Relenting.*) Good night, Alan. You're just a sentimental old monster, aren't you?

ALAN. Who, me?

JACQUELINE. Yes, you. Good night.

She goes out. ALAN, *left alone, lights a cigarette. Then he goes to door at back and opens it.*

ALAN. (*Calling.*) Jack?

JACQUELINE. (*Off.*) Yes?

ALAN. Will you see if Brian's in his room. I want to lock up.

JACQUELINE. (*Off.*) Right. (*After a pause.*) No, he must still be out.

ALAN. I'll leave a note for him.

He closes the door, takes an envelope from his pocket, and unscrews his pen. While he is writing, DIANA comes in softly and stands behind him. He doesn't hear her.

DIANA. (*Gently.*) Alan.

ALAN. (*Jumping up.*) Oh, God!

DIANA. Do you mind if I speak to you for a moment?

ALAN. (*Pointing vaguely at the ceiling.*) Well, I was just going to bed. (*Dashes to garden door.*)

DIANA. (*Inexorably.*) I suppose you didn't believe what I told you just now. (*She catches him.*)

ALAN. (*Looking despairingly round for help.*) No, I didn't believe it.

DIANA. (*With quiet resignation.*) No. I knew you wouldn't, and, of course, after what's happened I couldn't expect you to. But, whether you believe me or not, I just want to say this.

ALAN. (*Wildly.*) In the morning, Diana, say it in the morning. I'm frightfully tired and –

DIANA. Please listen to me. I just wanted to say that it's been you from the first moment we met. Kit and Bill never meant a thing to me. I let them think I was in love with them. But it was only because I had some idea it might make you jealous.

ALAN. It's a pity you didn't succeed.

DIANA. Oh, I know what you think of me, and you're quite right, I suppose. (*Pathetically.*) I've told so many lies before that I can't expect you to believe me when I'm telling the truth.

ALAN. Poor little Matilda.

DIANA. (*Comes back to* ALAN.) But this is the truth, now. This is the only completely sincere feeling I've ever had for anyone in all my life. (*Simply.*) I do love you, Alan. I always have and suppose I always will.

ALAN. (*In agony.*) Oh, go away. Please go away.

DIANA. All right. I know you have every right to think I'm lying, but I'm not, Alan, really, I'm not. That's what's so funny.

ALAN. (*Imploringly.*) Oh, God help me!

DIANA. (*At door.*) Good night, Alan. (*Simply.*) I do love you.

She smiles tearfully at him. He throws away his cigarette, and walks over to her.

ALAN. Say that again, blast you!

DIANA. I love you.

He embraces her fervently.

DIANA. (*Emerging from embrace, ecstatically.*) I suppose this is true.

ALAN. You know damn well it is.

DIANA. Say it, darling.

ALAN. (*Hedging.*) Say what?

DIANA. Say you love me.

ALAN. Must I? Oh, this is hell! (*Shouting.*) I love you.

DIANA. (*Turning back rapturously.*) Alan, darling –

BRIAN *comes in through window.*

BRIAN. Hello, Alan, hello, Diana, old thing.

DIANA *looks through* BRIAN *and turns hurriedly to the door.*

DIANA. (*Softly.*) Good night, Alan. I'll see you in the morning.

She goes out. ALAN *sinks into a chair.*

BRIAN. Did you see that, old boy? She cut me dead. She's furious with me. I must tell you about it, because it's a damned funny story. After you boys had gone I took Diana to have a bite of dinner with me. Well, we had a bottle of wine and got pretty gay, and all the time she was giving me the old green light.

ALAN. The green light?

BRIAN. Yes. The go-ahead signal. Well, after a bit I rather handed out an invitation to the waltz, if you follow me.

ALAN. Yes. I follow you.

BRIAN. I mean, everybody being out, it seemed an opportunity not to be missed. Well, do you know what she did then, old boy?

ALAN. No.

BRIAN. She gave me a sharp buffet on the kisser.

ALAN. What did you do?

BRIAN. I said, well, if that isn't what you want, what the hell do you want? Then she got up and left me. I never laughed so much in all my life.

ALAN. (*Dazedly.*) You laughed?

BRIAN. Wouldn't you, old boy?

> ALAN *gazes at him with amazed admiration.*

> Well, I'm for bed. I say, I met the most charming little girl just now on the front – fantastic piece she was. She gave me her card – yes, here it is. Colette, chez Mme Pontet, Rue Lafayette, 23. Bain 50 francs. I think I shall pop round tomorrow and have a bain.

ALAN. (*Rising and gazing at BRIAN with awe.*) Oh, Brian! How right-minded you are!

BRIAN. Me?

ALAN. Thank God you came in when you did. You don't know what you've done for me with your splendid, shining example. I now see my way clear before me. A great light has dawned.

BRIAN. I say, old boy, are you feeling all right?

ALAN. Listen, Brian. You weren't the only person to get the old green light from Diana tonight. I got it, too.

BRIAN. Doesn't surprise me. I should think she's pretty stingy with her yellows and reds.

ALAN. Yes, but I didn't respond to it in the same glorious way as you. However, what's done can be undone. (*Going to door.*) I am now going upstairs to put the same question to Diana that you did earlier in the evening.

BRIAN. I shouldn't, old boy. She'll say no, and believe me, she's got rather a painful way of saying it.

ALAN. If she says no, then, lacking your own sterling qualities, I shan't pay a visit to Rue Lafayette 23. No. I shall run away. I shall go back to London tomorrow.

BRIAN. But what about your exam and so forth?

ALAN. I shall chuck that. Well (*opening door*) I am now about to throw my future life into the balance of fate. Diplomat or writer. Which shall it be? Diana shall choose.

> ALAN *goes out.*

BRIAN. (*To himself.*) Crackers!

> *He shakes his head wonderingly. After a bit he rises, crosses to table, and stops to think.*

BRIAN. (*Musing*). Bain 50 francs! (*Fumbles for money and starts to count.*) Ten, twenty – thirty – forty – forty-one, forty-two – forty-three – forty-three – Damn.

Slamming of door is heard. ALAN *comes in.*

ALAN. I'm going to be a writer. Come and help me pack.

He disappears. BRIAN *follows him out murmuring expostulations as the curtain falls.*

Act Three, Scene Two

Scene: the same. Time: the next morning.

MARIANNE *is clearing away the breakfast,* JACQUELINE *helping her.* KENNETH *enters from window,* MAINGOT *following. They have evidently just finished a lesson.*

MAINGOT. (*At window.*) Dîtes à Monsieur Curtis que je l'attends. Il ne vaut pas la peine de continuer. Vous n'en saurez j'amais rien.

KENNETH. (*Sadly.*) Oui, Monsieur.

MAINGOT. Je serai dans le jardin. Oh, ma petite Jacqueline, que j'ai mal à la tête ce matin.

JACQUELINE. Pauvre, papa! Je suis bien fâchée.

MAINGOT. Ça passera – ça passera. Heuresement le quatorze ne vient qu'une fois par an.

He goes back into garden.

KENNETH. (*Calling.*) Brian.

BRIAN. (*Off.*) Yes, old boy?

KENNETH. Your lesson.

BRIAN. (*Off.*) Won't be a second.

KENNETH *closes the door and wanders mournfully over to the bookcase.*

JACQUELINE. Why so sad this morning, Kenneth?

KENNETH. You've heard the news about Alan.

JACQUELINE. Yes, my father told me.

KENNETH. Don't you think it s awful?

JACQUELINE. No. For one thing, I don't believe for a moment he's serious.

KENNETH. Oh, he's serious all right. What a damn fool! If I had half his chance of getting in the diplomatic I wouldn't go and chuck it up.

Enter BRIAN, *carrying a notebook.*

BRIAN. 'Morning all. Where's Maingot Père?

KENNETH. He's waiting for you in the garden.

BRIAN. Oh. (*Anxiously.*) Tell me, old boy, how is he this morning? Gay, happy – at peace with the world?

KENNETH. No. He's got a bad headache, and he's in a fiendish temper. (*He goes out.*)

BRIAN. Tut, tut. Couple of portos too many last night, I fear.

JACQUELINE. Why this tender anxiety for my father's health, Brian?

BRIAN. Well, Jack, I'm afraid I may have to deliver a rather rude shock to his nervous system. You see, I'm supposed to have done an essay on the Waterloo campaign, and what with one thing and another I don't seem to have got awfully far.

JACQUELINE. How far?

BRIAN. (*Reading.*) La bataille de Waterloo était gagnée sur les champs d'Eton.

JACQUELINE. And that's the essay, is it?

BRIAN *nods.*

Well, if I were you, I shouldn't show it to him. I'd tell him you did one of five pages and it got lost.

BRIAN. (*Doubtfully.*) Yes, but something seems to tell me he won't altogether credit that story.

Enter MAINGOT.

MAINGOT. Eh bien, Monsieur Curtis, qu'est-ce qu'on attend? Vous êtes en retard.

BRIAN. (*Affably.*) Ah, Monsieur, vous êtes bon – ce matin, j'espère?

MAINGOT. Non, j'ai affreusement mal à la tête.

BRIAN. (*Sympathetically.*) Oh. C'est trop mauvais. A trifle hungover, peut-être? Un tout petit peu suspendu?

MAINGOT. Vous êtes fou ce matin?

They go out together, MAINGOT *heard expostulating.*

BRIAN. (*Off, his voice coming faintly through the window.*) Il est très triste, Monsieur. J'ai perdu mon essai . . .

JACQUELINE *smiles. Having finished her clearing away, she takes off her apron and the handkerchief that covers her hair. She looks at herself in a pocket-mirror. The door at the back opens very slowly and* ALAN*'s head appears.*

ALAN. (*Whispering.*) Jack!

JACQUELINE. (*Turning.*) Hallo, Alan.

ALAN. Is Diana about?

JACQUELINE. She's in the garden. She wants to speak to you.

ALAN. I bet she does. But I'm taking good care she doesn't get a chance.

He comes cautiously into the room. He is dressed in a lounge suit preparatory for going away.

I want to get my books together. (*He goes to bookcase.*)

JACQUELINE. Alan, you're not serious about this, are you?

ALAN. Never more serious in my life, Jack. (*He is collecting books from the bookcase.*)

JACQUELINE. You're breaking Diana's heart, you know.

ALAN. Ha! Is that what she told you?

JACQUELINE. Oh, no. She wouldn't give herself away to me, but I honestly think she is rather in love with you, Alan.

ALAN. Yes, that's just what I'm afraid of.

JACQUELINE. You know, you're the only man in the world who's ever got away from Diana unscathed.

ALAN. (*Turning quickly.*) Don't say that! It's unlucky. I'm not out of the house yet.

He turns back to the bookcase as DIANA *comes quietly into the room from the garden.*

JACQUELINE. (*Quickly.*) Look out, Alan.

ALAN. (*Seeing* DIANA.) Oh, my God!

He darts out of the room, dropping all his books as he does so. DIANA *follows him out purposefully, but is too late. After a second she reappears.*

DIANA. It's no good, he's sure to have locked the door of his room. (*She sits down mournfully.*) I'm afraid he's quite determined to go. I feel dreadfully bad about it, because I'm responsible for the whole thing. All this talk of writing is just nonsense. He's only running away from me.

JACQUELINE. I don't altogether blame him.

DIANA. I suppose it's a wonderful compliment for a man to throw up his career just for my sake, but I can't see it that way. I'm really frightfully upset.

JACQUELINE. You don't look it.

DIANA. But I am, honestly I am. You see, I can't understand why he should want to run away from me. I can't see what he's got to be frightened of.

JACQUELINE. Can't you?

DIANA. If only I could get a chance to talk to him alone, I'm sure I could persuade him not to go.

JACQUELINE. I'm sure you could, too. So is Alan. But I don't think you'll get the chance.

Enter MARIANNE *from kitchen.*

MARIANNE. (*To* JACQUELINE.) S'il vous plaît, M'mselle, voulez vous venir voir la chambre de Lord Heybrook? Je l'ai préparée.

JACQUELINE. Bien, Marianne. Je viens tout de suite.

Exit MARIANNE, *and* JACQUELINE *follows her to the door.*

DIANA. Oh, does this Lord Heybrook arrive this morning?

JACQUELINE *has turned back to the kitchen door as the other door opens and* ALAN *comes in.* JACQUELINE *is momentarily alarmed for his safety, but sees* ROGERS, *who strolls in behind* ALAN, *and is reassured. She smiles and goes out.*

ALAN, *studiously avoiding looking at* DIANA, *goes over to the bookcase and picks up the books he has dropped.* ROGERS *takes a position between him and* DIANA, *nonchalantly looking up at the ceiling.*

DIANA. (*Quietly.*) Bill, please go away. I want to talk with Alan alone.

ROGERS. Well, it's . . .

DIANA. (*Shortly.*) Bill, did you hear me? I asked you to go.

ROGERS. (*Firmly.*) I'm sorry, I can't.

DIANA. (*Realising the situation, steps back with dignity.*) Do you think it's necessary to behave like this?

ALAN. You can say anything you want to say in front of Bill.

DIANA. No, thank you. I'd rather not.

ALAN. Then you don't say it.

DIANA. (*After a slight pause.*) All right, if you're determined to be so childish. This is all I want to say. (*With great sincerity.*) Alan, you know your own mind. If you feel you must run away from me, go ahead. I won't try to stop you. I only hope you'll be happy without me. I know I shan't be happy without you.

ALAN. (*Beginning to fall.*) You'll get over it.

DIANA. Oh, I expect so. You'll write to me occasionally, won't you?

ALAN. Oh, yes, every day, I expect.

DIANA. I'd like to know how you're getting on in your new career. I wish you the very, very best of luck.

ALAN. Thank you.

DIANA. I'll be thinking of you a lot.

ALAN. That's very kind of you.

DIANA. Well, that's really all I wanted to say, only . . . (*falteringly*) I would rather like to say goodbye, and that's a bit hard with Bill standing there like the Rock of Gibraltar.

There is a long pause.

ALAN. (*Suddenly.*) Bill, get out.

ROGERS *doesn't budge.*

ALAN. Get out, Bill.

ROGERS *seems not to have heard.* ALAN *approaches him menacingly.*

Get out, blast you!

ROGERS. (*Slowly.*) Is that the voice of reason, my dear fellow?

ALAN *stares at him and suddenly collects himself.*

ALAN. Oh, thank you, Bill. Come on, help me carry these books upstairs, and don't leave my side until I'm in that damned train.

They go towards the door.

DIANA. So you don't want to say goodbye?

ALAN. (*At door.*) Yes, I do. Goodbye.

He goes out, followed by ROGERS.

DIANA, *in a sudden rage, hurls some books through the door after them.*

DIANA. You forgot some.

She goes to kitchen door.

(*Calling.*) Marianne, à quelle heure arrive ce Lord Heybrook?

JACQUELINE. (*Calling from the kitchen.*) Lord Heybrook's arriving at ten-fifteen. (*She appears in the doorway.*) He'll be here any moment now.

DIANA. (*Annoyed.*) Oh, thank you very much.

JACQUELINE. Well, any luck with Alan?

DIANA. (*Shortly.*) No.

JACQUELINE. He wouldn't listen to reason?

DIANA. Do you mind, Jacqueline? I'm really too upset to talk about it.

JACQUELINE. Why don't you go to England with him, if you feel like that?

DIANA. How can I go chasing him across half a continent? One has a little pride after all.

JACQUELINE. Yes, I suppose one has.

DIANA. Besides, if Alan really feels he'll be happier without me, there's nothing I can do about it.

JACQUELINE. No, I suppose there isn't. (*Inconsequentially.*) Poor Lord Heybrook!

DIANA. What's Lord Heybrook got to do with it?

JACQUELINE. Nothing. (*She wanders over to the window.*) It's a lovely morning for a bathe, don't you think? There's a cold wind and the sea is rough, but I shouldn't let that stop you.

DIANA. Really, Jacqueline, you're becoming quite nice and catty in your old age. (*Defiantly.*) As a matter of fact, I think I will have a bathe. Why don't you come with me?

JACQUELINE. Oh, no. My bathing dress isn't nearly attractive enough. Besides, I'm giving lessons all the morning. (*Looking at her watch.*) I'm supposed to be giving one now. Kit's late as usual.

DIANA. By the way, how are you getting on in that direction?

JACQUELINE. Not very well, I'm afraid.

DIANA. Oh, I'm sorry. I suppose Kit's terribly upset about me?

JACQUELINE. You needn't worry. I shall do my best to console him.

DIANA. I've been horribly unkind to him. After Alan's gone I shall have to be specially nice to him to make up for it.

JACQUELINE. (*Alarmed.*) Oh, no.

DIANA *raises her eyebrows.*

Oh, why don't you go to England with Alan? Heaven knows Alan's never done me any harm, but I can feel quite ruthless about anything that will get you out of this house.

DIANA. Excitable race, you French – I always say.

Enter KIT.

KIT. (*Ignoring* DIANA.) Sorry, Jack. I'm late.

JACQUELINE. All right, Kit.

DIANA. Well, I don't want to disturb you. (*Going to door.*) I'm going to have a bathe.

DIANA *goes out.* KIT *stands shyly, holding a notebook.*

JACQUELINE. (*Adopting a schoolmistress manner.*) Sit down, Kit. Have you done that stuff?

They sit at table. KIT *hands her his notebook.*

Good. You must have worked quite hard.

She bends her head over the notebook. KIT *gazes at her.*

KIT. (*Suddenly.*) Jack, I want to say –

JACQUELINE. (*Hurriedly.*) This is wrong. (*She underlines a word.*) You can't say that in French. You have to turn it. (*She writes something in the book.*) Do you see?

KIT. (*Looking over her shoulder.*) Yes, I see.

JACQUELINE *continues to read.*

JACQUELINE. My dear Kit – (*Reading.*) Une pipe remplie avec du tabac. What ought it to be?

KIT. Remplie de tabac, of course.

JACQUELINE. Why didn't you write it, then? (*She underlines another word.*) Kit, this whole exercise is terrible. What on earth were you thinking of when you did it?

KIT. You.

JACQUELINE. Well, you'd better do it again.

KIT. (*Annoyed.*) What! Do it all again?

JACQUELINE. Yes. (*Weakening.*) Why were you thinking of me?

KIT. Not the whole damn thing?

JACQUELINE. Certainly. Why were you thinking of me?

KIT. (*With dignity.*) Shall I translate you some 'La Bruyère'?

JACQUELINE. All right.

KIT. Page one hundred and eight.

They take up their books in a dignified silence.

JACQUELINE. If I let you off, will you tell me?

KIT. I might.

JACQUELINE. Very well. You're let off. Only mind you, if you do another exercise as bad as that I'll make you do it again, and three more besides. Now, why were you thinking of me?

KIT. I was wondering whether I ought to tell you I was sorry for – for what happened last night, or whether I ought to pass it off with a gay laugh and a shrug of the shoulders.

JACQUELINE. Which did you decide?

KIT. I decided to leave it to you.

JACQUELINE. I think I'd rather have the gay laugh and the shrug of the shoulders.

KIT. You shall have it. (*He gets up.*)

JACQUELINE. No, you needn't bother. We'll take the gay laugh, etcetera, for granted.

KIT. (*Sitting.*) Very well. The incident is now closed, permanently and perpetually closed. (*He opens his book.*) Chapter four. Of love. There is a fragrance in pure friendship –

JACQUELINE. (*Puzzled at his attitude.*) I don't know why you should have thought I wanted you to apologise. After all what's a kiss between friends?

KIT. Alan told me this morning that you were in a steaming fury with me about it, so I thought –

JACQUELINE. Oh, I see. Alan's been talking to you about me this morning, has he? Come on, tell me, what's he been saying now?

KIT. I don't see why I shouldn't tell you. You see, last night, when Alan was a bit drunk, he played a stupid practical joke on me. He told me (*covering his face with his hands*) – this is a bit embarrassing, but it's a good laugh – he told me that you had been madly in love with me for two months. (*He uncovers his face and waits for the laugh, which doesn't come.*) Well, I, being also rather drunk, believed him, and so, as I was feeling rather sentimental, I – kissed you, as you remember; and of course I couldn't understand why you didn't fall into my arms and say, 'At last, at last!' or some such rot. However, this morning Alan told me the whole thing had been a joke, and that you were really rather angry with me for – well – spoiling a beautiful friendship, and all that nonsense. So that's why I thought I'd better apologise.

JACQUELINE. (*With sudden violence*.) What a blasted fool Alan is!

KIT. Yes, it was a damn silly trick to play. Not at all like him.

JACQUELINE. Kit – supposing I – had fallen into your arms and said, 'At last, at last!' or some such rot, what would you have done?

KIT. Oh, I should have kissed you again and said: 'I've loved you all the time without knowing it,' or some such idiocy.

JACQUELINE. Oh, Kit. You wouldn't.

KIT. (*Apologetically*.) Well, I told you I was feeling sentimental last night, and what with seeing what a fool I'd been over Diana and trying to forget her, and suddenly hearing that you were in love with me, and being drunk –

JACQUELINE. You don't feel sentimental this morning, do you?

KIT. Lord, no. You don't have to worry any more. I'm quite all right now.

He takes up his book and tries to concentrate.

JACQUELINE. Isn't there any chance of your feeling sentimental again, some time?

KIT. Oh, no. You're quite safe.

JACQUELINE. If I gave you a drink or two, and told you that what Alan said last night was the truth? And that I *have* been in love with you for two months and that I've been longing for you to kiss me every time I'm with you, would that make you feel sentimental?

KIT. There's no knowing what it mightn't make me feel.

Pause.

JACQUELINE. I haven't got any drink, Kit. Or must you have drink?

She stands up and KIT *embraces her.*

(*A little hysterically*.) At last! At last!

KIT. I've loved you all the time without knowing it.

JACQUELINE. Or some such idiocy.

KIT. I mean that, Jack.

JACQUELINE. Don't get serious, please, Kit. This is only a joke. It's only because we are both feeling a bit sentimental at the same time. (*Holding him away*.) Or are you?

KIT. Would I be behaving like this if I weren't?

JACQUELINE. I don't know. I wouldn't like to have played a sort of Diana trick on you. You haven't got that trapped feeling, have you?

KIT. I've got a peculiar feeling in the stomach, and an odd buzzing noise in the head. I think that must mean I'm in love with you.

JACQUELINE. You mustn't talk about love.

KIT. But you do.

JACQUELINE. I've got two months' start of you. I'm not going to let you mention the word 'love' for two months. Oh, Kit, do you think there's a chance you may be feeling sentimental in two months' time?

KIT. I'll take ten to one.

JACQUELINE. Well, go on being beastly to me in the meanwhile, because I should hate it if you didn't.

KIT. I'll try, but it won't be easy.

ALAN *pokes his head cautiously round the door.*

ALAN. Is Diana about?

JACQUELINE. Come in, Alan. You're quite safe, and I've got some news.

ALAN *comes in, followed by* ROGERS.

ALAN. What news?

JACQUELINE. I don't want the Commander to hear it. (*To* ROGERS.) Do you mind awfully?

ROGERS. Oh, no. Not at all. Tell me when you're finished.

He goes out.

ALAN. Well, what's the news?

JACQUELINE. Kit says it's just possible that in two months' time he may feel quite sentimental about me.

ALAN. Well, well, well. You could knock me over with a feather.

KIT. You've got a lot to explain, Alan. What the hell do you mean by telling me a whole packet of lies?

ALAN. Is that the proper way to speak to one, who, by a series of tortuous ruses, has at last brought you two love-birds together?

JACQUELINE. We're not love-birds. We're friends.

KIT. Sentimental friends.

JACQUELINE. No. Friends who sometimes feel sentimental.

ALAN. Well, make up your minds what you are, and I'll give you my blessing. Time presses. I came in to say goodbye.

ROGERS. (*Appearing in doorway.*) I can come in now, can't I?

JACQUELINE. How did you know?

ROGERS. Male intuition as opposed to female. I listened at the keyhole.

ALAN. Do you know, Jack, the only reason I'm sorry to be going is having to leave Bill just when I'd discovered him.

ROGERS. We'll see each other again, don't you worry. We're brothers under the skin.

ALAN. Tell me, Jack, did Diana say anything about coming to England with me?

JACQUELINE. No, she's definitely staying here. She says your happiness comes first.

ALAN. For my happiness read Lord Heybrook. Thank God for his lordship.

Enter KENNETH.

KENNETH. Alan, must you go?

ALAN. Yes, Babe, I must. There's a load off my mind, and I don't only mean Diana.

KENNETH. I don't think you know what you're doing.

ALAN. Oh, yes, I do.

A car noise is heard outside. MAINGOT *appears at window.*

MAINGOT. Jacqueline! Jacqueline! Je crois que c'est Lord Heybrook qui arrive. Es-tu-prête?

JACQUELINE. Oui, Papa.

MAINGOT. Bien! (*He darts out again.*)

JACQUELINE. (*Excitedly.*) Lord Heybrook! Oh, go and tell Diana, someone, or she'll miss her entrance.

KIT. (*Running to door.*) Diana, Lord Heybrook!

JACQUELINE. What does he look like, Kenneth?

KENNETH. I can't see. Your father is in the light.

ALAN. Oh, sit down, all of you. Give the man a chance.

MAINGOT. (*Calling off.*) Marianne! Les bagages!

Enter DIANA*, in her bathing dress. She takes up a position of nonchalance, with her back to the garden door.*

MAINGOT. (*Off.*) Par ici, Milord!

Enter LORD HEYBROOK *and* MAINGOT *from window.*

LORD HEYBROOK *is a bright young schoolboy, about fifteen years old.*

(*Escorting* LORD HEYBROOK *across the room.*) Alors vous êtes arrivé. J'espère que vous avez fait bon voyage . . . etc.

LORD HEYBROOK, *after smiling around shyly, goes out followed by* MAINGOT. JACQUELINE *collapses with laughter on* KIT*'s chest. The others begin to laugh also.*

DIANA. Come and help me pack, someone. I'm going to catch that London train or die.

She disappears through door at back.

ALAN. (*Pursuing her despairingly.*) No, no, oh, God, no! (*Turning at door.*) Stop laughing, you idiots. It isn't funny. It's a bloody tragedy.

But they only laugh the louder as the curtain falls.